JUEL ANDERSEN'S

CURRY PRIMER

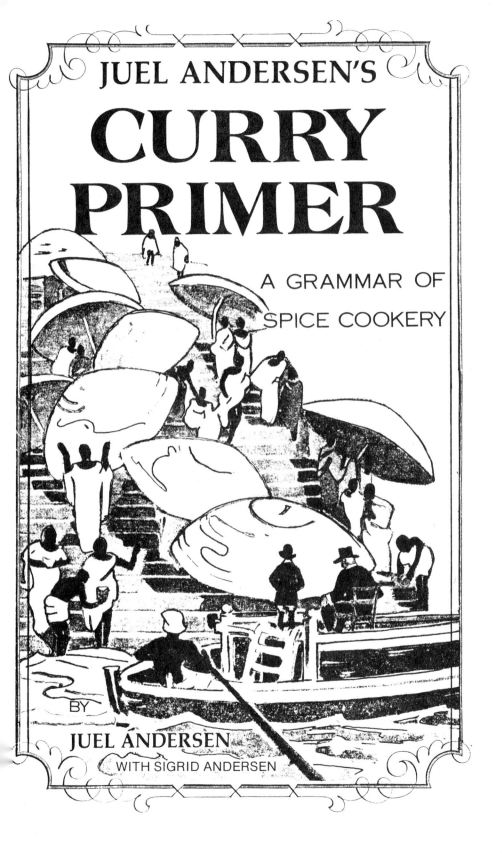

JUEL ANDERSEN'S
CURRY PRIMER

A GRAMMAR OF
SPICE COOKERY

BY
JUEL ANDERSEN
WITH SIGRID ANDERSEN

Illustrations from: *Adventures in Geography* by Gertrude Alice Kay, Wise-Parslow Company, New York. 1929. *Common School Geography*, Charles Scribner & Company, New York. 1871. *The Industrial Arts of India* by George Birdwood, Chapman and Hall, Ltd., London. 1873.

Book Design by Sigrid Andersen

ISBN 0-916870-79-0

Published by:
CREATIVE ARTS COMMUNICATIONS
833 Bancroft Way, Berkeley, California 94710

CONTENTS

TAJ MAHAL

WHAT CURRY IS AND WHAT IT IS NOT!

CURRY IS SPICY FOOD; CURRY IS COLORFUL FOOD. CURRY IS EXOTIC AND DELECTABLE FOOD. BUT THE CURRY WE HAVE ALWAYS KNOWN JUST DOESN'T EXIST.

BUT WE WILL CALL IT "CURRY" ANYWAY, AND SIMPLY REDEFINE IT. WE'LL SAY THAT IT IS SPICY BECAUSE IT IS PIQUANT, AROMATIC, TANGY, AND FLAVORFUL. IT IS NOT JUST PEPPERY AND "HOT."

WE WILL DESCRIBE IT AS COLORFUL FOOD, BECAUSE IT IS THE RED OF FRESH TOMATO AND PIMIENTO. IT IS THE GREEN OF PEAS, PARSLEY, AND GREEN PEPPER. IT IS THE WHITE OF YOGURT, FRESH CHEESE, AND RICE. IT IS THE YELLOW-ORANGE OF CARROTS AND SAFFRON, AND THE BROWN OF A RICH SAUCE.

IT IS EXOTIC BECAUSE IT IS UNUSUAL AND UNFAMILIAR; DIVERSE BECAUSE OF ITS ORIGINS IN A VAST NATION WITH A COMPLEX AND HETEROGE-NEOUS POPULATION, AND DELECTABLE BECAUSE IT IS WELL-PREPARED, WELL SEASONED, TEMPTING, AND DISTINCTIVE.

ABOUT THE WORD "CURRY"

BEFORE EUROPEANS ARRIVED IN INDIA NO DISH WAS CALLED CURRY. ENGLISHMEN LIVING IN INDIA BECAME ENAMORED OF THE EXOTIC FLAVORS OF THE NATIVE FOODS. THEY CALLED THESE PREPARATIONS "CURRY". THE WORD CAME TO DESCRIBE ALL INDIAN FOOD AND IT ENDURES TO THIS DAY.

IT MAY HAVE COME FROM THE TAMIL WORD KARI MEANING SAUCE, OR FROM THE NAME OF A SPICE CALLED KARI LEAF. IT MIGHT ALSO HAVE COME FROM THE NORTH INDIAN DISH KHARI, A KIND OF SPICY SOUP MADE OF BUTTERMILK AND CHICKPEA (GARBANZO) FLOUR. OR EVEN FROM THE WOK-LIKE, ALL-PURPOSE INDIAN COOKING POT CALLED A KARHAI.

INDIAN COOKERY ORIGINATES FROM SCORES OF COMMUNITIES, MAKES USE OF SPICES, HERBS, AND AROMATIC PLANTS IN UNIQUE AND IMAGINATIVE COMBINATIONS THAT DIFFER FROM REGION TO REGION, AND EVEN FROM COOK TO COOK. HOW COULD ONE WORD DESCRIBE SUCH DIVERSITY!

PERHAPS WHEN THIS KIND OF COOKING BECOMES MORE POPULAR SAYING "CURRY" WILL BECOME AS EMBARRASSING AS CALLING CHINESE FOOD "CHOP SUEY".

THROUGH TIME COMMERCIAL SPICE MIXTURES HAVE BECOME SO UNIFORM A BLEND THAT MOST OF US KNOW CURRIES ONLY AS YELLOW-COLORED FOODS WITH A STANDARD AROMA, OFTEN PEPPERY-HOT AND AS PREDICTABLE IN FLAVOR AS A BIG-MAC.

A LITTLE HISTORY

WHATEVER THIS KIND OF COOKING IS TO BE CALLED, COOKING WITH SPICES GOES BACK TO PRE-HISTORY.

GRINDING STONES FOUND IN EXCAVATIONS OF THE ANCIENT CITIES OF THE INDUS VALLEY, HARAPPA AND MOHENJODARO (4000 B.C.), CONTAINED TRACES OF MUSTARD SEED, CUMIN, SAFFRON, FENNEL, AND TAMARIND - WHICH, PRESUMABLY, WERE USED IN COOKING.

THESE CIVILIZATIONS WERE OVERRUN BY ARYANS FROM ASIA, WHO BROUGHT CATTLE WITH THEM, ADDING MILK, CURDS, AND BUTTER TO THE NATIVE FARE. BESIDES DAIRY FOODS, THEIR MOST NOTABLE CONTRIBUTION WAS THE "SHISH KEBAB" - SKEWERED

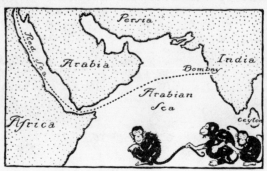

AND ROASTED CHUNKS OF MEAT- A TREAT THAT GOES
BY THAT NAME EVEN TODAY, ADDING UP TO ABOUT
3000 YEARS OF POPULARITY.

THE EARLY HOLY BOOK OF THE HINDUS, THE
"RIG-VEDA" (ABOUT 2000 BC.), BROKE WITH THE
ARYAN MEAT-EATING TRADITION BY ADVOCATING A
VEGETARIAN DIET AS A WAY OF ACHIEVING GREATER
SPIRITUAL ADVANCEMENT. THE EATING OF MILK
PRODUCTS WAS CONDONED; EATING PORK, FOWL, FISH,
AND EGGS WAS TOLERATED, BUT THE EATING OF
BEEF WAS FORBIDDEN.

LATER, THE BUDDHISTS, REVERENCING LIFE,
FROWNED ON KILLING ANIMALS FOR EATING,
ALTHOUGH THE
EATING OF AN
ANIMAL THAT WAS,
SAY, STRUCK BY
LIGHTING OR MET
OTHER MISFORTUNE
WAS OVERLOOKED.

THE INVASION OF
THE MOGHULS IN THE
MIDDLE AGES
BROUGHT ISLAM TO
INDIA. THEY WERE
MEAT-EATERS,
EATING BEEF, LAMB, GOAT, - ALL BUT PORK, WHICH
WAS FORBIDDEN THEM. THEIR CONTRIBUTION TO
INDIAN COOKING WAS CONSIDERABLE, ESPECIALLY
IN KASHMIR AND NORTH INDIA. THE MUGLAI
DISHES ARE SOME OF THE BEST, INCORPORATING
THE USE OF STRONG SPICES TO AN ALREADY
COMPLEX SET OF FLAVORS.

CHILI PEPPERS WERE BROUGHT TO INDIA BY
PORTUGUESE TRADERS IN THE 17TH CENTURY AND
WHOLEHEARTEDLY ADOPTED BY INDIANS WHO HAD
FORMERLY CONTENTED THEMSELVES WITH THE LESS
POTENT BLACK PEPPERCORNS WHICH ARE NATIVE TO
THEIR COUNTRY. THE ENTHUSIASM OF SOUTH
INDIANS FOR THESE ALARMING VIANDS STILL PERSISTS.

THE INVASION OF INDIA BY THE BRITISH BEGAN
IN 1600 AND BROUGHT MANY CHANGES AND INCIDENTS
RELATIVE TO FOOD. AS THE ULTIMATE CARNIVORES,
EATING ALL MANNER OF FLESH, THEY WERE NOTABLY

INSENSITIVE TO THE FOOD TABOOS OF MILLIONS OF SUBJECT PEOPLE.

THE SEPOY REBELLION WHICH STARTED IN 1857 AND DISRUPTED THE ENTIRE NATION BEGAN AS THE RESULT OF A RUMOR THAT THE NEW ENFIELD RIFLE SHELLS WERE PACKED IN A GREASE MADE OF BOTH COW AND PORK FAT, A SUBSTANCE THAT WOULD DEFILE HINDUS, SIKHS, AND MOSLEMS ALIKE.

THIS REBELLION BROUGHT INDIA UNDER THE BRITISH CROWN AS A COLONY AND THE KING BECAME THE EMPEROR OF INDIA. ENORMOUS NUMBERS OF ENGLISH MEN AND WOMEN WENT "OUT" TO INDIA.

AFTER LONG CAREERS, HOMEBOUND BRITAINS TOOK WITH THEM THE FLAVORS OF INDIA IN A SMALL, NEAT PACKET OF MIXED SPICES, ACCOMPLISHING THE CORRUPTION OF INDIAN CUISINE IN THE WESTERN WORLD, THE UBIQUITOUS AND MONOTONOUS CURRY POWDER FLAVOR WE KNOW TODAY.

RELIGION, ECONOMICS, AND VEGETARIAN COOKING

THE PREVALENCE OF ATTITUDES TOWARDS ANIMALS IN THE MAJOR RELIGIONS OF INDIA HAS IMBUED INDIAN CUISINE WITH SACRED AS WELL AS AMBROSIAL QUALITIES. VEGETARIANISM IS WIDESPREAD IN INDIA, CERTAINLY BECAUSE OF RELIGION, BUT ALSO BECAUSE OF ECONOMIC DEPENDENCE ON THE PRODUCTS OF THE COW. A COW'S MILK IS A MORE RENEWABLE SOURCE OF FOOD THAN ITS DEAD CARCASS.

MILK AND MILK PRODUCTS ARE MUCH PRIZED, MOST OFTEN IN PRESERVED FORMS. A BOILED-DOWN THICK MILK IS POPULAR AS ARE SOUR CURDS (YOGURT). A FRESH CHEESE IS MADE FROM PRESSED CURDS. BUTTER, BOILED AND CLARIFIED, IS CALLED **USLI GHEE** OR MERELY **GHEE** AND CAN BE KEPT FOR A LONG TIME WITHOUT REFRIGERATION.

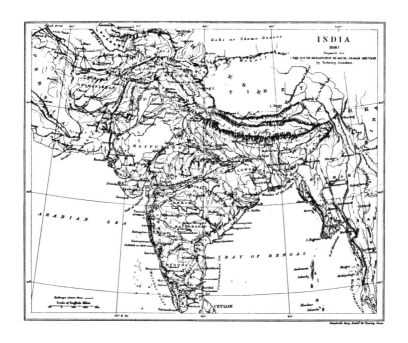

SOUTH INDIANS USE MUCH COCONUT AND COCONUT MILK AND THE MANGO IS OMNIPRESENT.

HIGH PROTEIN LEGUMES OF MANY KINDS ARE EATEN IN COMBINATION WITH RICE AND/OR WHEAT. ALL LEGUMES OR PULSES ARE CALLED **DHALL** AND CAN BE DRIED LENTILS, PEAS, OR BEANS OF MANY KINDS AND COLORS.

INDIAN VEGETARIAN COOKING IS INNOVATIVE AND WELL BALANCED NUTRITIONALLY. A MEAL WILL INCLUDE DHALL, RICE, VEGETABLES INCLUDING POTATOES, A VARIETY OF CONDIMENTS, AND DISHES MADE WITH CURDS. MILK DESSERTS ARE VERY POPULAR. ALL OF THESE FOODS ARE PREPARED WITH CARE AND IMAGINATION.

ABOUT CURRY SPICES

SPICING FOOD IS IDIOSYNCRATIC, EXPRESSING THE TASTES AND PERSONALITY OF THE COOK THROUGH THE SUBTLE COMBINATIONS USED. AS A FIRST STEP IN BECOMING FAMILIAR WITH THE SPICES USED IN CURRY LET'S LOOK AT THE LIST ON A STANDARD CAN OF CURRY POWDER.*

THE FIRST TWO ARE PROBABLY CORIANDER AND CUMIN. THIS IS BECAUSE CURRY POWDERS ARE MADE UP MOSTLY OF THESE TWO. NEXT MAY BE FENUGREEK, WHICH HAS THE STRONG AND DISTINCTIVE ODOR THAT YOU CAN SMELL RIGHT THROUGH THE TIGHTLY CLOSED CONTAINER.

THEN TURMERIC FOR COLOR, CHILIES FOR HEAT, AND A SELECTION FROM AMONG SUCH FAMILIARS AS CINNAMON, NUTMEG, MACE, GINGER, BLACK PEPPER, MUSTARD SEED, FENNEL, ANISE, CLOVE, BAY LEAF, CELERY SEED, AND CARDAMOM.

THE USE OF TURMERIC, FENUGREEK, AND CHILIES ALL GIVE COMMERCIAL CURRY POWDERS THEIR RECOGNIZABLE COLOR, DISTINCTIVE AROMA, AND TONGUE SHATTERING FIRE. NO MATTER WHAT ELSE THEY CONTAIN, THESE THREE ARE THE PARTIES RESPONSIBLE FOR THE SAMENESS OF FOODS SEASONED WITH COMMERCIAL "CURRY POWDER".**

BRANCH OF CLOVE-TREE.

THE MARVELOUS COMBINATIONS OF SPICES, HERBS, AND AROMATICS IN INDIAN USAGE ARE CALLED **MASALAS.** THEY DIFFER FOR THE FOOD TO BE COOKED AND THE STYLE OF THE COOKING. IT WOULD BE INCONCEIVABLE FOR AN INDIAN COOK TO USE THE SAME SPICES FOR EVERY PREPARATION.

MUSTARD (in Latin *sinapis*).

SOON YOU WILL BE MAKING YOUR OWN **MASALAS**. WITH SOME GUIDANCE FROM THE _CURRY PRIMER_, SOME KNOWLEDGE OF THE POSSIBILITIES, AND A LITTLE EXPERIENCE YOU WILL BE ASTONISHED AT THE RESULTS.

PEPPER.

* CURRY POWDERS HAVE BEEN DESCRIBED AND THUS STANDARDIZED BY THE U.S. DEPARTMENT OF AGRICULTURE IN A PUBLICATION CALLED _HANDBOOK NO. 8-2, COMPOSITION OF FOODS: SPICES AND HERBS (RAW, PROCESSED, PREPARED) REVISED JANUARY 1977._ THE DESCRIPTION IS AS FOLLOWS:

"CURRY POWDER"	%
CORIANDER	36
TURMERIC	28
CUMIN	10
FENUGREEK SEED	10
WHITE PEPPER	5
YELLOW MUSTARD	3
RED PEPPER	2
ALLSPICE	4
GINGER	2

** IT IS DOUBTFUL THAT THE U.S.P.A. CONSULTED ANY INDIAN CHEFS IN MAKING UP THIS STANDARD; NO DOUBT THEY CONSULTED SOME SPICE PROCESSING COMPANIES AND ARRIVED AT A CON ENSUS. SOME OTHER POPULAR MIXTURES FOLLOW.

SCHILLING CO. OR McCORMICK SPICE CO. LIST THEIR INGREDIENTS IDENTICALLY:
    CORIANDER, FENUGREEK, TURMERIC, CUMIN, BLACK PEPPER, BAY LEAF, CELERY SEED, NUTMEG, CLOVES, ONION, RED PEPPER, AND GINGER.

SPICE ISLANDS HAS CUMIN, CORIANDER, FENUGREEK, TURMERIC, DILL, AND CARDAMOM.

CROWN COLONY, THE SAFEWAY STORES BRAND OF SPICES, CONTAINS CORIANDER, TURMERIC, FENUGREEK, CUMIN, GINGER, RED PEPPER, BLACK PEPPER, CLOVES, CINNAMON, AND GARLIC.

SHIP BRAND FROM BOMBAY, INDIA LISTS CORIANDER SEEDS, TURMERIC, CHILLIES, CUMIN SEEDS, FENUGREEK SEEDS, FENNEL SEEDS, TRIFALA AND NAGKESER (FRAGRANT SPICES), CLOVES, CINNAMON, GARLIC, CURRY LEAVES, AND SALT.

CURRY ESSENTIALS
FOR NOVICES

THERE ARE A FEW THINGS YOU SHOULD
KNOW HOW TO MAKE IN ORDER TO BECOME A BETTER
CURRY COOK. YOU COULD BUY THEM, IF YOU COULD
FIND THEM, BUT MAKING THEM IS MORE FUN,
CHEAPER, AND WHAT WE ARE ABOUT IN THIS PRIMER.

#1 GHEE

USE ½ TO 1 POUND OF BUTTER

MELT THE BUTTER IN A SMALL HEAVY-BOTTOMED
SAUCEPAN AND BRING IT TO A BOIL, WATCHING
CAREFULLY TO SEE THAT IT DOES NOT BURN. (VERY
SLIGHT BROWNING IMPROVES THE FLAVOR.)

REDUCE HEAT AND ALLOW IT TO SIMMER OVER LOW
HEAT FOR A FEW MINUTES; SKIM THE FOAM FROM
THE TOP AS IT COOKS. COOL SOMEWHAT AND POUR
INTO A CROCK OR GLASS CONTAINER, BEING
CAREFUL TO KEEP BACK THE SEDIMENT THAT HAS
FORMED AT THE BOTTOM OF THE PAN.

GLAZED POTTERY, SINDH.

THIS IS USLI GHEE, THAT IS
REAL BUTTER. IT WILL KEEP WELL
AT ROOM TEMPERATURE FOR
QUITE A LONG TIME. USE IT
INSTEAD OF FRESH BUTTER OR
OIL FOR ALL SAUTEING AND
FRYING. AS THE MILK
SOLIDS ARE REMOVED, IT
WILL NOT BURN. MOST OF
THE SALT WILL HAVE STAYED
BEHIND WITH THE MILK SOLIDS.
OILS AND MARGARINES COOKED IN THIS WAY ARE
ALSO CALLED GHEE. THE PREFIX USLI IS RESERVED
FOR BUTTER.

#2 COCONUT MILK

THE SECOND ESSENTIAL IS COCONUT MILK. IT CAN

BE MADE FROM FRESHLY GRATED COCONUT, BUT THE MOST CONVENIENT WAY TO MAKE IT IS WITH DRIED, GRATED, UNSWEETENED COCONUT WHICH CAN BE PURCHASED IN BULK AT ANY NATURAL FOOD STORE.

2 CUPS GRATED, UNSWEETENED COCONUT
4 CUPS VERY HOT WATER

COMBINE COCONUT AND 2 CUPS OF WATER IN A BLENDER OR FOOD PROCESSOR AND BLEND AT HIGH SPEED FOR ABOUT A MINUTE. LET THE MIXTURE STAND AND COOL FOR ABOUT 15 MINUTES. LINE A COLANDER OR STRAINER WITH A MOISTENED, LOOSELY WOVEN, CLEAN CLOTH. PLACE THE COLANDER OVER A BOWL TO CATCH THE MILK AND POUR THE COCONUT MASH INTO THE CLOTH. PRESS AND SQUEEZE TO MAKE THICK COCONUT MILK.

RETURN THE COCONUT TO THE BLENDER. ADD ANOTHER 2 CUPS OF HOT WATER TO IT AND REPEAT THE PROCESS. MIX THE TWO BATCHES TOGETHER AND STORE IN A WIDE MOUTH JAR. DISCARD THE SOLID RESIDUE COCONUT.

THE COCONUT MILK WILL KEEP LESS THAN A WEEK. IF YOU WISH IT TO LAST LONGER, POUR IT INTO A POT AND HEAT IT TO 170° F., HOLDING IT AT THAT TEMPERATURE FOR 20 MINUTES. BOTTLE IT IN A STERILE CONTAINER WHILE STILL WARM.

WHEN MILK IS COLD YOU WILL FIND A LAYER OF HARD WHITE FAT ON THE TOP. THIS IS COCONUT OIL, WHICH IS HIGHLY SATURATED, THEREFORE BECOMES VERY HARD WHEN COLD.

#3 GARAM MASALA

THE THIRD ESSENTIAL IS A SPICE MIX THAT IS INVALUABLE. GARAM MASALA IS A COMBINATION OF SPICES USED TO FLAVOR MEATS AND VEGETABLES. IT IS GENERALLY ADDED TO FOODS NEAR THE END OF THE COOKING PERIOD, OR JUST BEFORE SERVING. THE DIRECT TRANSLATION IS "HOT SPICES"; YOU CAN ADJUST

THE DEGREE OF "HOTNESS" BY ADJUSTING THE AMOUNT
OF BLACK PEPPER USED.

IT IS GOOD TO KNOW THAT BLACK PEPPER BECOMES
HOTTER IF IT IS COOKED AND ALLOWED TO STAND. IF
IT IS SPRINKLED ON JUST BEFORE SERVING A DISH IT
WILL NOT BE SO HOT AND WILL BE DELIGHTFULLY
AROMATIC.

2	TEASPOONS CARDAMOM
1 TO 2	TEASPOONS BLACK PEPPERCORNS, TO TASTE
1	TBSP. CUMIN SEEDS
2	TEASPOONS CORIANDER SEEDS
8	WHOLE CLOVES
2	TEASPOONS BLACK OR YELLOW MUSTARD SEEDS
1	2" CINNAMON STICK, CRUSHED

PREHEAT OVEN TO 250°F. SPREAD THE SPICES ON A
BAKING PAN AND TOAST FOR ABOUT 15 MINUTES.
WHEN COOL, GRIND THEM IN A COFFEE GRINDER, SPICE
GRINDER, PEPPER MILL, BAMIX, MORTAR AND PESTLE,
OR A COFFEE MILL.* STORE IN A TIGHTLY CLOSED
CONTAINER.

THIS RECIPE MAKES ABOUT 4 TABLESPOONS OF
GARAM MASALA. YOU CAN MAKE MORE, IF YOU WISH,
BUT IT LOSES PIQUANCY WHEN STORED TOO LONG.

IF YOU WOULD LIKE TO CHANGE THE CHARACTER
OF YOUR CURRIES BUT WOULD LIKE THE CONVENIENCE
OF READY-MIX SPICES, THE THING TO DO IS TO MAKE
UP A CURRY POWDER OF YOUR OWN.

#4 CURRY POWDER

YOU CAN CHOOSE THE SPICES YOU LIKE MOST AND DELETE
THOSE SPICES THAT YOU DO NOT CARE FOR. THEN YOU
CAN USE IT IN ANY RECIPE THAT CALLS FOR "CURRY
POWDER" AND ADD OTHER SPICES AT WILL. I PARTIC-
ULARLY LIKE THE FOLLOWING COMBINATION OF
SPICES, WHICH CUTS DOWN ON FENUGREEK, TURMERIC,
AND HOT PEPPERS.

PREHEAT OVEN TO 250° F.

3 TBSP. CORIANDER SEEDS
1 TBSP. CUMIN SEEDS
1 TBSP. MUSTARD SEEDS
6 WHOLE CLOVES
1 1" PIECE OF STICK CINNAMON, CRUSHED
1/2 TEASPOON FENNEL OR ANISE SEEDS
1/2 TEASPOON BLACK OR WHITE PEPPERCORNS
1/2 TEASPOON CARDAMOM SEEDS

1/2 TEASPOON CELERY SEED
3 TO 10 WHOLE FENUGREEK SEEDS, TO TASTE
2 TBSP. CORIANDER (GROUND)
1 TEASPOON POWDERED GINGER
1/4 TEASPOON GROUND NUTMEG
1 TEASPOON TO 2 TBSP. GROUND TURMERIC, AS YOU WISH
1/8 TEASPOON CAYENNE PEPPER
2 TEASPOONS PAPRIKA

COMBINE THE WHOLE SPICES IN A PAN AND BAKE FOR 15 MINUTES, IN A 250°F OVEN, STIRRING FREQUENTLY.

NUTMEG-TREE AND FRUIT.

COOL. COMBINE WITH THE RESERVED POWDERED SPICES AND GRIND WITH A BLENDER, COFFEE GRINDER*, BAMIX, OR SPICE MILL. STORE IN A TIGHTLY CLOSED CONTAINER; A JAR IS BEST. MAKES ABOUT 1/2 CUP.

* IF YOU USE A COFFEE GRINDER TO GRIND SPICES, DO NOT USE IT FOR COFFEE, TOO, ELSE YOUR COFFEE WILL TASTE LIKE CURRY! A SPARE COFFEE GRINDER IS VERY HANDY TO GRIND SMALL AMOUNTS OF GRAINS AND SPICES AND TO CHOP NUTS.

THE GRAMMAR OF
SPICE COOKERY

TO BREAK WITH "CURRY POWDER" AND BRANCH INTO USING THE SPICES INDIVIDUALLY, CAN BE QUITE CONFUSING. YOU MIGHT WONDER HOW YOU WILL EVER LEARN WHAT THE SPICES ARE AND WHICH ARE PROPER TO WHAT FOODS.

THE ANSWER TO PROPER IS THAT THE WORD JUST DOESN'T APPLY. CERTAIN SPICES ARE BETTER WITH SOME FOODS THAN WITH OTHERS AND THAT IS LARGELY A MATTER OF TASTE. AS FOR LEARNING THE SPICES, IF YOU COOK AT ALL, YOU KNOW MOST OF THEM ALREADY. A LITTLE EXPERIENCE WITH THE NEW ONES AND MORE USE OF THE ONES YOU ALREADY KNOW IS ALL YOU NEED.

INDIAN FOOD IS SPICY FOOD; SPICY SHOULD NOT BE CONSTRUED AS HOT. HOT IS PEPPERY. IN DEFERENCE TO THOSE AMONG US (INCLUDING ME) WHO CANNOT ABIDE BLISTERING FOOD, HOT PEPPER (CHILIES, CAYENNE, ETC.) HAS BEEN MADE AN OPTIONAL INGREDIENT IN MOST OF THE RECIPES.

FENUGREEK IS ANOTHER OPTIONAL SPICE. IT IS THE SPICE THAT MAKES ALL CURRIES SMELL ALIKE. THIS IS WHY I USE IT SPARINGLY, IF AT ALL; YOU CAN USE IT IF YOU LIKE IT.

TURMERIC IS MOSTLY A COLORING AGENT AND ADDS LITTLE TO THE FLAVOR. IF YOU DO NOT LIKE YELLOW FOOD, YELLOW APRONS, YELLOW BLUE JEANS, YELLOW UTENSILS, AND A YELLOW COUNTER TOP, IT CAN BE LEFT OUT.

THE SPICING OF FOOD SHOULD RESULT IN A BLEND OF FLAVORS IN WHICH NO ONE FLAVOR DOMINATES. IT SHOULD BE A MEDLEY, NOT A CACOPHONY. (OR BETTER, A CACOFLAVY!)

PLANNING AND GETTING STARTED

TO HELP YOU BECOME ACCUSTOMED TO PLANNING AND COOKING CURRY MEALS, THE RECIPES IN THE CURRY PRIMER ARE ARRANGED IN MENUS. EACH MEAL IS PLANNED FOR FOUR PEOPLE. THE MENU IS

FOLLOWED BY A GLOSSARY OF THE NAMES OF THINGS THAT MAY BE UNFAMILIAR. OTHER UNFAMILIAR TERMS CAN BE FOUND IN THE DICTIONARY AT THE BACK OF THE BOOK.

THE SELECTION OF RECIPES DOES NOT FOLLOW THE CUISINE OF ANY ONE AREA; THEY ARE A GATHERING OF GOOD DISHES FROM LOTS OF PLACES. RECIPES HAVE BEEN ADAPTED FOR COOKING IN WESTERN KITCHENS WITH COMMON WESTERN UTENSILS.

SHOPPING

IT IS GREAT FUN TO SPEND SOME TIME IN AN EAST ASIAN GROCERY STORE, IF THERE IS ONE IN YOUR TOWN. THERE WILL BE MANY THINGS YOU CANNOT FIND ELSEWHERE, SUCH AS WHITE POPPY SEED, BLACK MUSTARD SEED, AND MANGO POWDER.

ON THE OTHER HAND, MOST OF THE THINGS YOU NEED IN ORDER TO COOK A PERFECT CURRY ARE RIGHT IN YOUR NEARBY SUPERMARKET. FAMILIAR MEATS, SEAFOODS, POULTRY, VEGETABLES, AND FRUITS ARE THE BASICS.

MOST OF THE WHOLE SEEDS AND SPICES ARE ALSO AVAILABLE IN ORDINARY GROCERY STORES. IF YOU CAN'T FIND THEM THERE, YOU WILL CERTAINLY FIND THEM IN YOUR LOCAL NATURAL FOOD STORE.

SO IF YOU ARE NOT 100% AUTHENTIC IN YOUR SHOPPING, PLEASE DON'T WORRY ABOUT IT. YOU CAN DO A WONDERFUL JOB IN YOUR VERY OWN AMERICAN KITCHEN, WITH YOUR WONDERFUL APPLIANCES, YOUR EXCELLENT EQUIPMENT AND YOUR MODERN COOKSTOVE. JUST DON'T BREATHE IT TO A SOUL!

COOKING UTENSILS

THE ONLY SPECIAL COOKING EQUIPMENT I SUGGEST IS A WOK. BECAUSE IT HAS A SMALL

BOTTOM AND A LARGE COOKING SURFACE, LESS FAT IS NEEDED FOR FRYING. INDIANS USE A SIMILAR UTENSIL CALLED A **KARHAI**.

IT IS ALSO HANDY TO HAVE AN IRON SKILLET OR TWO. THESE ARE VERY INEXPENSIVE AND GOOD FOR ALL KINDS OF COOKING. OTHER ORDINARY COOKWARE IS ALL THAT IS NECESSARY.

METHODS

THE ONE OUTSTANDING METHOD IN INDIAN COOKING IS WHAT IS CALLED **BHOON** AND THAT TRANSLATES SIMPLY TO "FRY". ALMOST ALL INDIAN FOOD IS COOKED ON TOP OF THE STOVE. WE WOULD CALL THE METHOD "STIR-FRYING" OR "SAUTEING" WHICH MEANS THAT FOOD IS COOKED IN AS LITTLE FAT AS POSSIBLE, AND IS STIRRED ATTENTIVELY WHILE IT COOKS.

ONE UNIQUE FEATURE OF INDIAN COOKING IS THAT ALL SPICES ARE COOKED IN ONE WAY OR ANOTHER, EITHER BAKED, BROILED, OR FRIED. THIS BRINGS OUT THE FLAVORS AND PREVENTS A RAW TASTE.

SERVING

AN INDIAN MEAL IS COMPOSED OF SEVERAL DISHES SERVED ALL AT THE SAME TIME, WITH THE EXCEPTION OF DESSERTS WHICH IMMEDIATELY FOLLOW THE MEAL. THIS MAKES SERVING EASY.

A TYPICAL MENU INCLUDES ANYWHERE FROM JUST ONE MAIN MEAT OR VEGETABLE DISH TO SEVERAL, DEPENDING ON THE NUMBER OF PEOPLE TO BE SERVED. THERE WILL BE AT LEAST ONE RICE DISH AND/OR A LEGUME DISH. A COLD VEGETABLE, RAW OR COOKED, WILL BE MARINATED IN YOGURT OR SOUR CURDS. THESE WILL BE ACCOMPANIED BY VARIOUS APPETIZERS, CONDIMENTS AND BREAD.

SOUP IS NOT CUSTOMARY WITH INDIAN MEALS. THE FAMILIAR "INDIAN" SOUP, **MULLIGATAWNY** IS A

HYBRID OF CURRY SPICES AND VEGETABLE/MEAT STOCK, WITH ADDED EDIBLES. IT IS MOST ENCHANTING AND SATISFYING, BUT IT DOES NOT ORDINARILY ACCOMPANY AN INDIAN MEAL.

THE FOODS ARE ALWAYS BITE-SIZED. SOME ARE MEANT TO BE EATEN WITH THE FINGERS. OTHERS, THE SAUCED ONES, YOU WILL PROBABLY PREFER TO EAT WITH A FORK OR SPOON. BREAD ACTS AS HELPER; AS PUSHER, SCOOPER, AND WRAPPER. ONLY WATER IS SERVED WITH THE MEAL; WINE IS A WESTERN INNOVATION. DESSERT IS A SWEET, FRUIT AND/OR A MILK PUDDING AND THE BEVERAGE: TEA.

TEA DRINKING WAS INTRODUCED TO INDIA BY THE BRITISH IN THE LAST CENTURY. IT WAS FOUND THAT NORTH INDIA HAD WILD TEA TREES WHICH FAR SURPASSED THE CHINESE TEAS THE ENGLISH HAD BEEN ACCUSTOMED TO. INDIANS TOOK TO TEA WITH ENTHUSIASM AND IT IS ALL BUT THE FAVORITE NATIONAL DRINK BY NOW. ORANGE PEKOE, THE FAVORITE TEA OF AMERICANS, COMES FROM DARJEELING, INDIA.

THE MEALS CAN BE SERVED AS A BUFFET OR AS A SIT DOWN MEAL. YOU MIGHT TRY SITTING ON CUSHIONS ON THE FLOOR, AROUND A LARGE COFFEE TABLE- FOR THE FUN OF IT. IMAGINE YOURSELF AS BEING EAST INDIAN, RELAX AND ENJOY THE EXOTIC FLAVORS; SAVOR EACH DISH INDIVIDUALLY; DO NOT USE KETCHUP*.

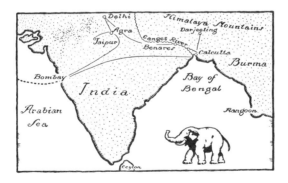

* THE WORD "KETCHUP" COMES FROM THE SIAMESE WORD "KACHIAP". THE SAUCE SEEMS TO HAVE MADE ITS WAY TO ENGLAND VIA CHINA, SOUTHEAST ASIA, AND INDIA.

Recipes For

MENU 1

KOFTA CURRY

BROCCOLI and RICE
with
CUMIN SEEDS

PEAS and POTATOES

PARATHAS

CUCUMBER RAITA

KHEER

GLOSSARY

KOFTA — MEAT BALLS USUALLY OF LAMB OR BEEF, GROUND AND MIXED WITH ONIONS, GARLIC, GINGER, AND SPICES AND SERVED IN A CURRY SAUCE. THE SPICES IN THE FOLLOWING RECIPE COULD BE CALLED A "KOFTA MIXTURE" AND CAN BE USED WITH OTHER MEATS, FLAKED FISH, OR WITH MASHED TEMPEH.

PARATHA — A FLAT BREAD MADE WITH BUTTER AND LAYERED WITH FLAVORINGS. IT IS ESPECIALLY DELICIOUS AND QUITE EASY TO MAKE.

RAITA — A DISH MADE OF COOKED OR UNCOOKED VEGETABLES AND YOGURT OR SOUR CURDS. A SORT OF SALAD, IT IS SERVED ALONG WITH THE OTHER DISHES OF THE MEAL.

KHEER — A PUDDING MADE OF THICK MILK AND RICE, SERVED COLD.

KOFTA CURRY

KOFTAS

1 1/2	LBS. GROUND MEAT	1	TBSP. YOGURT
1	SMALL ONION, CHOPPED	1/2	TEASPOON SALT, OR TO TASTE
1	CLOVE GARLIC, MINCED	A	DASH OF HOT PEPPER (OPTIONAL)
1	TEASPOON **GARAM MASALA**	1/4	CUP **GHEE** FOR FRYING
1	EGG		

COMBINE ALL INGREDIENTS IN A BOWL AND BEAT UNTIL CREAMY. THIS CAN BE DONE IN A FOOD PROCESSOR WITH THE STEEL BLADE, WITH A ROTARY BEATER, OR BY HAND.

HEAT THE GHEE IN A WOK OR SKILLET. FORM 1" BALLS WITH A SPOON AND FRY A FEW AT A TIME, SHAPING THEM WITH A FORK AS YOU COOK ALL SIDES. WHEN FIRM, BUT ONLY LIGHTLY BROWNED, REMOVE WITH A SLOTTED SPOON TO A PLATE COVERED WITH PAPER TOWELS TO DRAIN EXCESS OIL.

SAUCE

1	TBSP. CORIANDER
1/2	TEASPOON TURMERIC
1	TEASPOON MUSTARD SEED, BLACK PREFERRED
1	TEASPOON CUMIN
1	TEASPOON PAPRIKA
1/2	TEASPOON GROUND GINGER
A	DASH OF CAYENNE OR HOT PEPPER, TO TASTE
1	LARGE ONION, THINLY SLICED
3	CLOVES GARLIC, THINLY SLICED
2	CUPS THIN COCONUT MILK <u>OR</u> 1 CUP ANY MILK DILUTED WITH 1 CUP WATER
1/8	OF A LEMON WITH RIND, CUT IN PIECES
1/2	TEASPOON SALT, OR TO TASTE

COMBINE THE SPICES AND GRIND THEM TO A POWDER. SET ASIDE. POUR OFF THE FRYING OIL, LEAVING ABOUT 3 TABLESPOONS IN THE PAN. FRY THE ONIONS AND GARLIC OVER MEDIUM HEAT UNTIL SOFTENED. ADD THE GROUND SPICES AND STIR WITH THE ONIONS FOR

ABOUT 3 MINUTES.
ADD THE COCONUT MILK AND LEMON CHUNKS, STIR WELL, AND BRING TO A BOIL. TASTE THE SAUCE AND ADD SALT, IF NEEDED. TRANSFER THE MEATBALLS TO A CASSEROLE OR SAUCEPAN. POUR THE SAUCE OVER THEM AND CONTINUE TO COOK, OVER MEDIUM TO LOW HEAT FOR ABOUT ONE-HALF HOUR UNTIL SAUCE IS REDUCED AND THICKENED.

BROCCOLI and RICE with CUMIN SEEDS

3	1" STALKS BROCCOLI
1-2	TBSP. OIL
2	TBSP. WATER
A	DASH OF SALT AND PEPPER, TO TASTE
2	TBSP. USLI GHEE
1/2	TEASPOON CUMIN SEEDS
1	CUP RICE
1 1/2	CUPS BOILING WATER
1/2	TEASPOON SALT, OR TO TASTE

CLEAN THE BROCCOLI. CUT OFF THE STEMS AND PEEL THEM, REMOVING THE FIBROUS COVERING. CUT THE STEMS INTO 1" PIECES AND SEPARATE THE FLOWERETS INTO BITE-SIZED PIECES. HEAT THE OIL IN A WOK AND STIR AND FRY THE BROCCOLI FOR A MINUTE OR TWO. ADD THE WATER (2 TBSP.), COVER AND STEAM FOR ABOUT 5 MINUTES. SALT AND PEPPER TO TASTE AND SET ASIDE UNTIL RICE IS READY. (THE BROCCOLI CAN BE PREPARED MUCH AHEAD OF TIME, IF DESIRED.)
HEAT THE USLI GHEE IN A HEAVY-BOTTOMED PAN THAT CAN BE COVERED TIGHTLY. FRY THE CUMIN SEEDS IN THE GHEE FOR ABOUT 2 MINUTES. ADD THE RICE AND STIR AND FRY FOR A MINUTE MORE. POUR IN THE BOILING WATER AND ADD THE SALT. LOWER THE HEAT, COVER AND COOK FOR ABOUT 10 MINUTES, ADDING MORE WATER IF NECESSARY.

CONTINUED

ARRANGE THE BROCCOLI OVER THE TOP OF THE RICE. COVER AND COOK ANOTHER 10 MINUTES OR SO, UNTIL RICE AND BROCCOLI ARE DONE.

CAREFULLY TRANSFER THE RICE AND BROCCOLI TO A SERVING DISH.

THIS WAY OF PREPARING RICE AND A VEGETABLE IS EXCELLENT WITH ANY CRUCIFEROUS — AND THEREFORE FLAVORFUL— VEGETABLE: CAULIFLOWER, CABBAGE, BRUSSEL SPROUTS, KALE, KOHLRABI, OR ANY OTHER.

PEAS and POTATOES

3 LARGE OR 5 MEDIUM POTATOES (ABOUT 1 LB.)	1/2 TEASPOON SALT, OR TO TASTE
1 SLICE FRESH GINGER (SIZE OF A HALF DOLLAR)	1/3 CUP WATER
1/2 TEASPOON GROUND TURMERIC	2 TEASPOONS LEMON JUICE
2 TBSP. WATER	1 TBSP. CHOPPED JALAPEÑO OR OTHER HOT GREEN PEPPER, OPTIONAL
2 TBSP. OIL	
1 TEASPOON GROUND CUMIN	1 TBSP. CHOPPED CILANTRO OR PARSLEY
1 TEASPOON GROUND CORIANDER	1/2 TEASPOON **GARAM MASALA**

WASH AND CUBE POTATOES INTO 3/4" PIECES; DO NOT PEEL THEM, UNLESS NECESSARY. SET THEM ASIDE IN A BOWL OF COLD WATER.

COMBINE THE GINGER AND TURMERIC IN A BLENDER WITH THE 2 TBSP. WATER AND CHOP UNTIL GINGER IS VERY FINE.

HEAT THE OIL IN A WOK AND FRY THE CUMIN AND CORIANDER FOR A MINUTE OR TWO. ADD THE GINGER/ TURMERIC MIXTURE AND THE WELL DRAINED POTATOES. STIR AND FRY FOR FIVE MINUTES OR SO.

ADD THE SALT, WATER, AND LEMON JUICE. COVER AND COOK UNTIL THE POTATOES ARE DONE AND THE WATER HAS EVAPORATED. WHEN POTATOES ARE FULLY COOKED CAREFULLY STIR IN JALAPEÑO, PARSLEY, AND GARAM MASALA. ITS NOW READY TO SERVE.

PARATHAS

DOUGH

1 1/2 CUPS WHOLE WHEAT PASTRY FLOUR
1/2 CUP UNBLEACHED ALL-PURPOSE FLOUR
1/2 TEASPOON SALT (OPTIONAL)
2 TBSP. OIL
1/2 CUP WARM WATER

SIFT FLOURS AND SALT TOGETHER INTO A BOWL OR INTO THE FOOD PROCESSOR. WORK IN THE OIL AND THEN ADD WATER TO MAKE A SOFT DOUGH WHICH LEAVES THE SIDES OF THE BOWL. KNEAD FOR SEVERAL MINUTES ON A FLOURED BOARD. RETURN TO THE BOWL, COVER AND ALLOW THE DOUGH TO STAND FOR AN HOUR OR SO.

FILLING AND BAKING

PARATHAS CAN BE ROLLED OUT AND BAKED UNFILLED OR THEY CAN BE FILLED WITH SPICES, ONIONS, GARLIC OR WHATEVER YOU LIKE. THIS RECIPE IS FOR GARLIC FILLING, BUT VARY AT WILL.

6 CLOVES GARLIC, VERY FINELY CHOPPED
COARSELY GROUND BLACK PEPPER
1/4 CUP MELTED USLI GHEE

DIVIDE THE DOUGH INTO 6 PARTS. ROLL EACH INTO A 9" CIRCLE. BRUSH WITH MELTED GHEE OR BUTTER AND SPRINKLE WITH GARLIC AND BLACK PEPPER. (GARAM MASALA IS ALSO IN ORDER, IF YOU WISH) ROLL

CONTINUED

EACH ROUND INTO A CYLINDER AND THEN COIL IT TIGHTLY.
ROLL COIL INTO A 7" ROUND. EVEN IF YOU ARE USING
NO FILLING, THE PARATHAS SHOULD BE ROLLED,
BUTTERED, COILED, AND ROLLED AGAIN BEFORE BAKING.
BAKE ON A HEAVY GRIDDLE OVER MEDIUM HEAT. THE
PAN SHOULD BE LIGHTLY BUTTERED WITH USLI GHEE.
    STORE THE PARATHAS IN FOIL OR PLASTIC
WRAP UNTIL READY TO SERVE. RE-HEAT IN THE
FOIL OR A DAMP CLOTH AND SERVE HOT.

FILLING VARIATIONS

- POPPY SEEDS
- MUSTARD SEEDS
- GARAM MASALA
- CHOPPED ONION OR SCALLION
- CHOPPED JALAPENO
- SESAME SEEDS
- CINNAMON AND SUGAR
- RAISINS
- CARDAMOM SEED
- COMBINATIONS OF THE ABOVE

CUCUMBER RAITA

1	MEDIUM CUCUMBER	1/2	TEASPOON CUMIN
1	CUP PLAIN YOGURT		SALT AND BLACK PEPPER
1/2	TEASPOON CELERY		TO TASTE
	SEED		PAPRIKA AND PARSLEY

    WASH, PEEL, AND CUT THE CUCUMBER INTO
QUARTERS, THEN IN 1/4" CHUNKS. BEAT THE YOGURT
WITH THE CELERY SEED, CUMIN, SALT, AND PEPPER
WITH A SMALL WHIP OR A FORK, UNTIL CREAMY. FOLD
IN THE CUCUMBER. GARNISH WITH PAPRIKA AND
CHOPPED PARSLEY.
    THIS SHOULD BE THE LAST THING YOU MAKE BEFORE
SERVING THE MEAL. IF IT STANDS THE CUCUMBER WILL
WEEP AND THE RAITA WILL BE WATERY.

KHEER

1	QUART WHOLE MILK	2	TBSP. HONEY OR MAPLE SUGAR (TO TASTE)
1	TBSP. LONG GRAIN WHITE RICE*		
5	CARDAMOM SEEDS	A	PINCH OF SALT
1	1" STICK OF CINNAMON	12	SLIVERED ALMONDS (BLANCHED)

COMBINE THE MILK, RICE, CARDAMOM, CINNAMON, AND SALT IN A HEAVY SAUCE PAN. BRING TO A BOIL, REDUCE HEAT AND SIMMER SLOWLY UNTIL VOLUME IS REDUCED TO 2 CUPS. STIR OFTEN TO PREVENT BURNING OR BROWNING.

ADD THE HONEY, SALT, AND COOK, STIRRING, FOR ANOTHER FEW MINUTES. IT SHOULD BE THE CONSISTENCY OF VERY THICK CREAM.

REMOVE THE CINNAMON STICK; ADD THE ALMONDS, POUR INTO A GLASS BOWL AND SERVE WARM OR CHILLED. DUST WITH CINNAMON AND GARNISH WITH A LITTLE FRESH FRUIT.

PHYSICAL CHARACTER OF ASIA.

* WHITE RICE MUST BE USED TO GET THE PROPER VELVETY TEXTURE IN THIS DISH. CONVERTED RICE OR BROWN RICE WILL NOT WORK WELL. IF YOU WISH TO USE BROWN RICE, IT MUST BE THE SWEET, GLUTINOUS KIND.

Recipes For

MENU 2

CHICKEN TOMATO CURRY

COCONUT RICE

ZUCCHINI BOORTHA

CHAPATTIS

SWEET LEMON PICKLE

SPINACH RAITA

FRIED BANANAS

GLOSSARY

BOORTHA ~ A BOORTHA IS A VEGETABLE PREPARATION MADE WITH VARIOUS SPICES, SEEDS, AND AROMATICS SUCH AS ONIONS, AND GARLIC. IT IS NOT A CURRY, BUT SHARES SOME OF THE CURRY ATTRIBUTES.

CHAPATTI ~ A FLAT BREAD SIMILAR TO A MEXICAN FLOUR TORTILLA, GENERALLY MADE OF WHOLE-WHEAT FLOUR. IT IS BAKED ON A GRIDDLE, SERVED WARM, AND USED AS A SCOOP FOR SAUCED FOODS. SEE THE RECIPE ON PAGE 54.

RAITA ~ VEGETABLE SALAD WITH YOGURT.

SPICE-BOX OF MORADABAD WORK.

CHICKEN TOMATO CURRY

MARINADE

1	3 LB. FRYER OR 2 LEGS WITH THIGH AND 1 WHOLE BREAST
4 OR 5	CLOVES GARLIC
1	3/4" CUBE FRESH GINGER
1/4	CUP PLAIN YOGURT
4	MEDIUM-SIZED FRESH TOMATOES, PEELED AND CHOPPED
1	LARGE ONION, CHOPPED
1	TBSP. GROUND CORIANDER
2	TEASPOONS PAPRIKA
1	TBSP. CHOPPED FRESH PARSLEY OR CILANTRO
1/2	TEASPOON SALT OR TO TASTE

CUT THE CHICKEN INTO SERVING PIECES AND REMOVE THE SKIN AND EXCESS FAT. THE BREAST WILL MAKE FOUR PIECES AND EACH WHOLE LEG WILL MAKE TWO. PLACE IN A BOWL.

PEEL THE GARLIC AND CHOP THE GINGER INTO SMALL PIECES. COMBINE THESE IN A BLENDER WITH THE YOGURT AND BLEND TO A PASTE.

COMBINE THE YOGURT PASTE, TOMATOES, ONION CORIANDER, PAPRIKA, PARSLEY, AND SALT IN A BOWL AND MIX WELL. POUR THIS MARINADE OVER THE CHICKEN, STIR WELL AND SET ASIDE FOR AT LEAST ONE HOUR.

PREPARATION

1/4 TO 1/2	CUP GHEE, FOR FRYING
1/8	TEASPOON CARDAMOM SEEDS
1	2" CINNAMON STICK
1/4	TEASPOON GROUND CLOVES

HEAT 1/4 CUP GHEE OR OIL IN A WOK. FRY THE SPICES FOR A MINUTE OR TWO. DRAIN CHICKEN PIECES AND FRY THEM, TWO OR THREE AT A TIME IN THE GHEE, REMOVE THEM TO A CASSEROLE AS THEY BROWN AND FRY THE OTHER PIECES. DON'T TRY TO FRY ALL THE CHICKEN AT ONCE. ADD MORE GHEE IF NECESSARY; WHEN THE FRYING IS FINISHED, POUR OFF THE FRYING FAT, IF ANY REMAINS. REMOVE THE WHOLE SPICES AND DISCARD THEM.

ADD THE MARINADE TO THE PAN AND BRING TO A SIMMER. POUR THIS OVER THE CHICKEN IN THE CASSEROLE. PLACE UNCOVERED IN A PRE-HEATED 350°F. OVEN FOR ABOUT 25 MINUTES, UNTIL THE CHICKEN IS DONE. SERVE.

COCONUT RICE

1	TBSP. USLI GHEE OR OIL	2	CUPS COCONUT MILK
2	TBSP. CHOPPED ONIONS	1/2	TEASPOON SALT, OR TO TASTE
1 1/2	CUPS ANY RICE		WATER AS NEEDED

HEAT THE GHEE IN A HEAVY SAUCE PAN THAT HAS A TIGHT COVER. FRY THE ONIONS LIGHTLY, UNTIL SOFTENED. ADD THE RICE AND STIR AND FRY FOR A MINUTE. ADD THE COCONUT MILK, SALT AND ENOUGH WATER TO COVER THE RICE BY ABOUT 1 INCH. BRING TO A BOIL, REDUCE HEAT, COVER AND SIMMER SLOWLY UNTIL ALL THE MOISTURE IS ABSORBED. ADD WATER, IF NEEDED, DURING THE COOKING.

BUDDHISTIC COPPER VASE,

WITH DETAIL OF GRAVEN DECORATION.

ZUCCHINI BOORTHA

2	LARGE OR 4 MEDIUM ZUCCHINI	1/2	TEASPOON GROUND GINGER
1	TBSP. GHEE	1/2	TEASPOON SALT, OR TO TASTE
1	SMALL ONION, CHOPPED	1	TBSP. COOKED JALAPEÑO OR HOT GREEN PEPPER (OPTIONAL)
1	SMALL CLOVE GARLIC, CHOPPED		
1/2	TEASPOON GROUND CUMIN		

WASH, QUARTER, AND CUT ZUCCHINI INTO 1/4" SLICES. HEAT THE GHEE IN A WOK. ADD THE ONION, GARLIC, CUMIN, AND GINGER AND STIR AND FRY FOR A MINUTE OR TWO.

ADD THE ZUCCHINI, STIR UNTIL IT IS COATED WITH OIL AND SPICES. REDUCE HEAT, COVER TIGHTLY AND ALLOW TO STEAM, WITHOUT WATER UNTIL ZUCCHINI IS COOKED TO YOUR LIKING. MIX WITH THE JALAPEÑO OR OTHER HOT PEPPER, TO TASTE.

SWEET LEMON PICKLE

SO GOOD YOU WILL EAT IT ON TOAST FOR BREAKFAST!

MAKES 1 CUP

1	LARGE LEMON
1	EACH, SMALL SWEET RED AND GREEN PEPPER
1	SMALL ONION
2	TBSP. RAISINS
1/3	CUP WATER
1/2	TEASPOON CORIANDER SEED
1/2	TEASPOON CUMIN SEED
1	1/2" STICK CINNAMON
1	TEASPOON MUSTARD SEED, BLACK PREFERRED
1/3	CUP HONEY OR **JAGGERY**
1	TBSP. VINEGAR
HOT PEPPER TO TASTE	
1/2	TEASPOON SALT, OR TO TASTE

CUT THE LEMON, WITH PEEL, INTO 8 SECTIONS. REMOVE SEEDS AND CUT EACH SECTION INTO 4 PIECES. SEED AND CUT THE PEPPERS INTO CHUNKS ABOUT THE SAME SIZE AS THE LEMON PIECES. CUT THE ONION THE SAME WAY. COMBINE THE CHOPPED FOODS WITH THE RAISINS AND WATER IN A HEAVY BOTTOMED SAUCEPAN.

COMBINE AND GRIND THE SPICES COARSELY. ADD THESE TO THE SAUCEPAN. COOK UNTIL THE PEPPER AND ONIONS ARE "AL DENTE", THAT IS, NOT TOO SOFT. ADD THE HONEY OR JAGGERY, VINEGAR, SALT, AND HOT PEPPER AND COOK UNTIL THE LIQUID IS SYRUPY. COOL AND BOTTLE; STORE IN THE REFRIGERATOR.

GLAZED [SILICIOUS] POTTERY, IN WHITE AND BLUE, OF DELHI.

CONTINUED

THIS CONDIMENT SHOULD BE A LITTLE **HOT** TO BE AT ITS BEST, SO EXPERIMENT. REMEMBER, YOU CAN ADD PEPPER BUT YOU CAN'T TAKE IT OUT!

SPINACH RAITA

1	CUP COOKED, CHOPPED SPINACH OR OTHER GREENS	1	TEASPOON BLACK MUSTARD SEEDS
1	TEASPOON **USLI GHEE**	1	CUP PLAIN YOGURT
1	TEASPOON CUMIN SEEDS		SALT AND PEPPER, TO TASTE
			CAYENNE PEPPER, IF DESIRED

HEAT THE GHEE IN A SMALL SKILLET UNTIL IT IS MELTED. FRY THE MUSTARD AND CUMIN SEED UNTIL MUSTARD BEGINS TO POP. MIX THIS WITH THE SPINACH.

BEAT THE YOGURT WITH SALT, PEPPER, AND CAYENNE. ADD TO THE SPINACH AND MIX LIGHTLY AND WELL WITH A FORK. REFRIGERATE UNTIL READY TO SERVE.

GLAZED POTTERY, SINDH

FRIED BANANAS

1	TBSP. LEMON JUICE	A	DASH OF FRESHLY GROUND NUTMEG
1/2	CUP ORANGE JUICE	4	LARGE, ALMOST RIPE BANANAS
2	TBSP. HONEY OR JAGGERY OR BROWN SUGAR	1/4	CUP USLI GHEE
1/2	TEASPOON GROUND CINNAMON	1	CUP PLAIN YOGURT

MIX THE JUICES, HONEY, AND SPICES. PEEL

AND CUT THE BANANAS IN HALF, THEN CUT EACH HALF
IN TWO, LENGTHWISE.

MELT THE GHEE IN A LARGE, HEAVY SKILLET.
POUR IN THE JUICE MIXTURE AND THEN ARRANGE THE
BANANAS. COOK UNTIL ALL MOISTURE IS EVAPORATED
AND THE BANANAS BECOME SOFT AND BROWN. SERVE
HOT WITH YOGURT.

Recipes For

MENU 3

KHEEMA

EGGPLANT MOLEE

DHALL CURRY

NAN

TOMATO-ONION RAITA

RASGULLA

DHALL (DAL) — LEGUMES SUCH AS LENTILS, PEAS, GARBANZOS, BEANS PREPARED WITH CURRY SPICES AND SERVED AS A HIGH PROTEIN FOOD WITH VEGETARIAN AND NON-VEGETARIAN MEALS.

KHEEMA — THE WORD MEANS "GROUND MEAT". IT ALSO REFERS TO A STEWLIKE CURRY MADE WITH GROUND MEAT OF ANY KIND.

MOLEE — ANY DISH COOKED WITH A SAUCE MADE WITH COCONUT MILK.

NAN — ONE OF THE VERY FEW LEAVENED BREADS MADE IN INDIA. IT IS TRADITIONALLY BAKED IN A **TANDOOR**, WHICH IS A CLAY OVEN USED IN THE PUNJAB OF NORTH INDIA. IT IS STUCK ON THE WALLS OF THE INSIDE OF THE TANDOOR. TANDOOR COOKS, IT IS SAID, CAN BE RECOGNIZED BY THEIR HAIRLESS ARMS; THE HAIR IS BURNED OFF FROM REACHING INTO THE TANDOOR TO RETRIEVE NAN.

RASGULLA — A DELICIOUS AND VERY SWEET CONFECTION, FLAVORED WITH ROSEWATER AND MADE WITH HOME MADE CHEESE. IT IS VERY POPULAR IN ALL OF INDIA.

KHEEMA

2	TBSP. **GHEE** OR OIL	1 1/2	LBS. GROUND MEAT
1	LARGE ONION, CHOPPED	2	LARGE POTATOES, CUT INTO 1/4" CUBES
3	CLOVES GARLIC, CHOPPED	1/2	TEASPOON SALT, OR TO TASTE
1	3/4" CUBE FRESH GINGER, CHOPPED FINE		CAYENNE PEPPER, TO TASTE (OPTIONAL)
1	TBSP. PAPRIKA	1/8	LEMON, CHOPPED WITH SKIN
1	TBSP. GROUND CUMIN	1/4	CUP YOGURT
1	TBSP. GROUND CORIANDER	1/4	CUP TOMATO SAUCE
1/2	TEASPOON GROUND TURMERIC		WATER, AS NEEDED
		1/4	TEASPOON MACE
1/2	TEASPOON GROUND CLOVES	1	TEASPOON **GARAM MASALA**
1/4	TEASPOON GROUND CINNAMON	2	TBSP. CHOPPED JALAPEÑO OR HOT GREEN PEPPER

HEAT GHEE OR OIL IN A WOK. ADD THE ONIONS, GARLIC, AND GINGER AND STIR AND FRY UNTIL ONIONS ARE SOFTENED. ADD THE SPICES AND MIX WELL WITH THE ONIONS, STIRRING AND FRYING FOR ANOTHER MINUTE OR TWO. ADD THE GROUND MEAT AND FRY UNTIL MEAT IS SOMEWHAT BROWNED, STIRRING FREQUENTLY.

STIR IN THE CUBED POTATOES, SALT, CAYENNE, LEMON PIECES, YOGURT, AND TOMATO SAUCE. ADD ABOUT 1/4 TO 1/3 CUP WATER, AS NEEDED TO KEEP THE KHEEMA MOIST. COVER AND COOK UNTIL THE POTATOES ARE DONE.

ADD THE MACE, GARAM MASALA, AND HOT PEPPER, IF YOU ARE USING IT. SERVE AT ONCE.

EGGPLANT MOLEE

1	MEDIUM EGGPLANT	1/4	SMALL SWEET GREEN PEPPER
～	OIL		
1	MEDIUM ONION	1	TBSP. **GHEE**
1	CLOVE GARLIC		SALT TO TASTE
2	THIN SLICES FRESH GINGER	1	CUP COCONUT MILK
1	JALAPEÑO OR HOT GREEN PEPPER, TO TASTE		

TRIM THE ENDS FROM THE EGGPLANT AND SLICE 1" THICK. COAT EACH SIDE WITH OIL, USING THE FINGERS. ARRANGE ON A BAKING SHEET AND COOK UNDER THE BROILER UNTIL EACH SIDE IS DARK BROWN AND THE EGGPLANT IS SOFT. REMOVE FROM THE OVEN AND SET ASIDE.

SLICE THE ONION AND GARLIC VERY THIN. REMOVE THE SEEDS FROM THE HOT PEPPER AND SWEET PEPPER AND SLICE VERY THIN AS WELL.

HEAT THE GHEE IN A HEAVY FRYING PAN. SAUTÉ THE SLICED VEGETABLES UNTIL THEY ARE SOFTENED. ADD THE SALT AND COCONUT MILK AND BRING TO A SIMMER. ARRANGE THE EGGPLANT SLICES IN THE PAN AND SPOON THE SAUCE OVER THEM. COOK UNTIL THE SAUCE DISAPPEARS AND THE MOLEE SEEMS QUITE DRY. THIS CAN BE DONE IN A 350°F. OVEN WHILE YOU PREPARE OTHER DISHES FOR THE MEAL.

DHALL CURRY

1 1/2	CUPS DRY LENTILS
1	SMALL ONION, CHOPPED
2	CLOVES GARLIC, CHOPPED
1	BAY LEAF
1	1" CINNAMON STICK
3	CUPS WATER

COMBINE ALL INGREDIENTS IN A HEAVY BOTTOMED SAUCEPAN. BRING TO A BOIL. LOWER HEAT, COVER LOOSELY AND SIMMER UNTIL THE LENTILS ARE TENDER, BUT NOT TOO SOFT. STRAIN, RESERVING THE COOKING LIQUID, AND REMOVE BAY LEAF AND CINNAMON STICK.

YOU CAN SERVE THE LENTILS JUST THIS WAY OR
GO ON AND FINISH THEM AS FOLLOWS:

2	TBSP. OIL
2	TBSP. CHOPPED ONION
6	WHOLE CARDAMOM SEEDS
1	TEASPOON PAPRIKA
1	TEASPOON BLACK MUSTARD SEED
1/2	TEASPOON TURMERIC
1	TBSP. TOMATO SAUCE

SALT TO TASTE

HEAT THE OIL IN A WOK.   STIR AND FRY THE ONIONS
UNTIL THEY ARE SOFTENED.   ADD THE CARDAMOM,
PAPRIKA, MUSTARD SEED, AND TURMERIC AND COOK FOR
A MINUTE OR TWO.   ADD THE DRAINED
LENTILS, TOMATO SAUCE AND
ENOUGH LENTIL WATER TO SUIT
YOU.   IT CAN BE WET WITH
SAUCE OR DRY
WITHOUT SAUCE,
AS YOU LIKE.
SIMMER UNTIL THE
LENTILS AND ONIONS
ARE AS SOFT AS
DESIRED.

NAN

MAKES 6 TO 8 SMALL LOAVES

1	CUP WHEY OR BUTTERMILK	3	CUPS WHOLE WHEAT PASTRY FLOUR OR
2	TBSP. USLI GHEE		UNBLEACHED
1/2	TEASPOON SALT, OPTIONAL		ALL-PURPOSE FLOUR OR ANY
1	TEASPOON HONEY		MIXTURE OF THE
2	EGGS		TWO
1	TBSP. DRY ACTIVE YEAST		

HEAT THE WHEY OR BUTTERMILK WITH THE
GHEE, ONLY ENOUGH TO MELT THE FAT.   TRANSFER
TO A BOWL OR TO A FOOD PROCESSOR AND COOL TO
LUKEWARM.   BEAT IN THE SALT, HONEY, EGGS, AND
YEAST.   ADD THE FLOUR A 1/2 CUP AT A TIME,

CONTINUED

BEATING AS LONG AS YOU CAN AND THEN KNEADING IN THE REST, MAKING A SOFT, ELASTIC AND SHINY DOUGH.

PLACE IN A GREASED BOWL, COVER WITH A TOWEL AND ALLOW TO RISE UNTIL DOUBLED IN BULK. HEAT THE OVEN TO 450° F. AND PUT THE EMPTY PANS YOU PLAN TO USE INTO THE OVEN TO HEAT. IF YOU HAVE ANY CAST IRON PANS LARGE ENOUGH, THEY ARE BEST.

ROLL THE DOUGH INTO A LONG CYLINDER ON A FLOURED PASTRY BOARD. CUT THE CYLINDER INTO 6 OR 8 EQUAL PIECES. MAKE A FLATTENED, OVAL CAKE OF EACH PIECE. BRUSH EACH WITH MELTED GHEE. ALLOW THEM TO STAND ON THE PASTRY BOARD FOR ABOUT 20 MINUTES.

CARRY THE PASTRY BOARD TO THE OVEN. CAREFULLY TRANSFER THE CAKES TO THE HEATED PANS WITH A PANCAKE TURNER. WORK QUICKLY.

BAKE THE BREADS FOR 6 TO 10 MINUTES, UNTIL FIRM TO THE TOUCH. PLACE ON A RACK. SERVE HOT OR AT ROOM TEMPERATURE.

TOMATO-ONION RAITA

3	MEDIUM TOMATOES	1	TEASPOON **GARAM MASALA**
1	SMALL RED ONION OR 5 SCALLIONS	1/2	TEASPOON SALT, OR TO TASTE
1	TBSP. GRATED COCONUT	1	CUP UNFLAVORED YOGURT
2	TBSP. FRESH PARSLEY OR CORIANDER, CHOPPED		

WASH AND CUT THE TOMATOES INTO QUARTERS. SQUEEZE EACH TO REMOVE SEEDS. CHOP INTO SMALL PIECES.

CHOP THE ONION OR CUT SCALLIONS IN 1/4" ROUNDS, USING THE GREEN PART AS WELL.

TOSS ALL INGREDIENTS IN A BOWL AND THEN MIX WITH THE YOGURT. REFRIGERATE UNTIL SERVED.

RASGULLA

1/2	CUP **PANEER** (RECIPE PAGE 47)	A	PINCH OF CREAM OF TARTAR
1	TBSP. SEMOLINA FLOUR	3	CUPS WATER
1/2	TEASPOON BAKING POWDER	1	TEASPOON ROSEWATER (OPTIONAL)
1	CUP HONEY OR JAGGERY		LEMON SLICES
			YOGURT

KNEAD THE CHEESE (PANEER) ON A MARBLE OR IN A SHALLOW STAINLESS STEEL PAN FOR ABOUT 5 MINUTES. MIX THE SEMOLINA AND BAKING POWDER WELL AND GRADUALLY KNEAD THIS INTO THE CHEESE, A LITTLE AT A TIME, USING THE HEEL OF THE HAND IN A SLIDING MOTION ACROSS THE MARBLE OR PAN. THE CHEESE WILL BECOME SOFT AND RATHER STICKY. SCRAPE IT UP AND REFRIGERATE IT WHILE YOU COOK THE SYRUP.

ALL THIS CAN BE DONE VERY NICELY AND QUICKLY IN A FOOD PROCESSOR, IF YOU HAVE ONE. CREAM THE CHEESE AND ADD THE SEMOLINA GRADUALLY, BEATING FOR ONE OR TWO MINUTES AFTER THE ADDITIONS. REFRIGERATE.

MIX THE HONEY, CREAM OF TARTAR, AND WATER AND BOIL FOR A FEW MINUTES TO MAKE A LIGHT SYRUP.

MAKE ABOUT 20 BALLS, ABOUT 3/4" IN DIAMETER, AND PLACE THEM IN THE BOILING SYRUP BY PLACING EACH ON A SPOON AND SUBMERGING THE SPOON IN THE SYRUP. BRING THE SYRUP BACK TO A BOIL AND COVER THE PAN. REDUCE THE HEAT AND ALLOW THE DUMPLINGS TO BOIL FOR ABOUT 20 MINUTES.

CHECK THEM OFTEN. IF THE SYRUP IS REDUCED SO THAT THE DUMPLINGS ARE NOT COVERED, ADD ONE OR TWO TABLESPOONS OF WATER.

REMOVE THE COOKED DUMPLINGS VERY CAREFULLY WITH A SLOTTED SPOON AND ARRANGE IN A FLAT DISH LIKE A SOUP BOWL. ADD WATER TO THIN THE SYRUP LEFT IN THE PAN, ADD THE ROSEWATER TO THIS SYRUP AND POUR OVER THE DUMPLINGS. COOL TO ROOM TEMPERATURE AND REFRIGERATE.

SERVE TWO OR THREE OF THESE VERY SWEET DUMPLINGS WITH A SLICE OF LEMON OR LIME AND A DAB OF YOGURT.

Recipes For

MENU 4

```
(A feast for 8 to 12 people)
KHARI with PAKORI
BIRIANI
MADRAS EGG CURRY
PEAS with PANEER
CHAPATTIS
MIXED VEGETABLE RAITA
CARROT HALWA
```

GLOSSARY

BIRIANI — A FESTIVE, AND REGAL RICE DISH, TRADITIONAL AMONG NORTH INDIANS. IT INVOLVES MAKING AT LEAST THREE SEPARATE DISHES AND COMBINING THEM INTO A MAGNIFICENT WHOLE, GARNISHED AT WILL WITH NUTS, RAISINS, DATES, FRUIT, AND GOLD OR SILVER FOIL. IT IS COMPARABLE TO THE SPANISH "PAELLA" IN COMPLEXITY.

CHAPATTIS — FLAT BREAD, SEE RECIPE PAGE 54.

HALWA — A PUDDING OR A MORE SOLID CONFECTION MADE OF GRAIN, SEEDS, OR VEGETABLES.

KHARI — A THICK PORRIDGE-LIKE SOUP MADE OF CHICK PEA (GARBANZO) FLOUR.

PANEER — A FRESH CHEESE SIMILAR TO RICOTTA OR COTTAGE CHEESE.

PAKORI — A DEEP-FRIED DUMPLING MADE WITH CHICK PEA (GARBANZO) FLOUR.

KHARI with PAKORI

KHARI

1/2	CUP GARBANZO FLOUR	1/2	TEASPOON CELERY SEEDS
1	QUART BUTTERMILK	1/4	TEASPOON FENNEL SEEDS
2	CUPS WATER	1/8	TEASPOON FENUGREEK SEEDS (OPTIONAL)
1	TBSP. GHEE		
1	TEASPOON BLACK MUSTARD SEEDS	1/2	TEASPOON SALT, OR TO TASTE
1/2	TEASPOON CUMIN SEEDS		CAYENNE, TO TASTE

COMBINE THE GARBANZO FLOUR AND 1 CUP OF BUTTERMILK AND BEAT UNTIL VERY SMOOTH.

MELT THE GHEE AND FRY THE SEEDS UNTIL THE MUSTARD SEEDS POP A BIT. ADD THE WATER, 3 CUPS OF BUTTERMILK, AND THE GARBANZO MIXTURE AND STIR UNTIL WELL MIXED AND SMOOTH. BRING TO A BOIL, THEN REDUCE HEAT AND SIMMER FOR ABOUT 30 MINUTES.

PAKORI

2/3	CUP GARBANZO FLOUR
1/3	CUP WHOLE WHEAT FLOUR
1	TEASPOON BAKING POWDER
1/2	TEASPOON SALT, TO TASTE
1	TEASPOON CHOPPED PARSLEY
1	TBSP. DRY CHOPPED ONIONS
1/2	TEASPOON GROUND CUMIN
1/4	CUP COARSELY CHOPPED PEANUTS
1/4	TEASPOON COARSELY GROUND BLACK PEPPER
1/3-1/2	CUP WATER
1/2	CUP OIL, FOR FRYING

MIX ALL THE INGREDIENTS EXCEPT OIL IN A BOWL. ADD ENOUGH WATER AND BEAT TO MAKE A THICK BATTER, TOO MOIST TO HANDLE, BUT NOT POURABLE.

HEAT THE OIL IN A WOK. DROP THE DUMPLINGS BY TEASPOONSFUL INTO THE HOT

CONTINUED

OIL. FRY GENTLY, TURNING OFTEN. WHEN THEY
ARE GOLDEN (NOT BROWNED) REMOVE WITH A SLOTTED
SPOON AND DRAIN ON A PAPER TOWEL. COOK THEM
ALL AND SET ASIDE.
BEFORE SERVING TIME, ADD PAKORI TO THE
SIMMERING SOUP AND COOK TOGETHER FOR 10
MINUTES.

BIRIANI

RICE

SERVES 6

4	CUPS WATER	1	TEASPOON SALT
8	EACH: PEPPERCORNS, CLOVES, CARDAMOM SEEDS	1 1/2	CUPS CONVERTED RICE
		1	TEASPOON PAPRIKA
1	1" STICK CINNAMON	1	TEASPOON TURMERIC

BRING THE WATER TO A BOIL WITH THE
SPICES AND SALT. ADD THE RICE AND
COOK FOR 10 MINUTES. DRAIN IN A
LARGE STRAINER INTO A SAUCEPAN.
PICK OUT THE CINNAMON STICK AND
THE OTHER SPICES, IF YOU WISH.
BRING THE COOKING WATER TO A
BOIL AND REDUCE TO 1 CUP. ADD THE
PAPRIKA AND TURMERIC AND STIR WELL.
SET ASIDE.

VEGETABLES

1	LARGE ONION, CHOPPED COARSELY	1	TEASPOON CURRY POWDER (RECIPE PAGE 17)
2	TBSP. GHEE	1	10 OZ. PACKAGE FROZEN PEAS
1	3/4" CUBE OF FRESH GINGER, CHOPPED	2	TBSP. WATER
5	CLOVES GARLIC, CHOPPED	1/4	CUP CHOPPED SWEET RED AND GREEN PEPPER
2	TEASPOONS POPPY SEED	3	TBSP. RAISINS
1/2	TEASPOON CUMIN SEED		

HEAT THE GHEE IN A WOK AND STIR/
FRY ONIONS UNTIL THEY BEGIN TO
BROWN. ADD THE GINGER AND GARLIC
AND COOK A FEW MINUTES LONGER.
STIR IN THE POPPY SEED, CUMIN
SEED, AND CURRY POWDER AND
CONTINUE TO COOK FOR A
MINUTE OR TWO.
    ADD THE PEAS AND WATER
TO THE WOK AND COOK UNTIL THE
PEAS ARE THAWED. STIR IN THE
PEPPERS AND RAISINS; REMOVE FROM
FROM HEAT, SET ASIDE.

OTHER FILLINGS

    THE BIRIANI IS READY FOR ASSEMBLY NOW. TO
MAKE IT INCREASINGLY COMPLICATED YOU CAN USE
A FILLING OF **KORMA** (RECIPE PAGE 52) OR **KHEEMA**
(RECIPE PAGE 37 , KOFTA (RECIPE PAGE 24) OR
CHICKEN (PAGE 31).
    I OFFER HERE A SIMPLE TWO-PURPOSE RECIPE FOR
SOMETHING UNEXPECTED, A TUNA FISH FILLING THAT
IS ALSO A WONDERFUL TUNA SALAD.

1	CAN WATER PACKED TUNA (7 OZ. CAN)
1/2-1	TEASPOON **GARAM MASALA**
1	TEASPOON LEMON JUICE
1	TBSP. TOMATO SAUCE
2	TBSP. YOGURT

FLAKE TUNA AND MIX WITH THE
OTHER INGREDIENTS.

ASSEMBLY OF BIRIANI

    PREHEAT OVEN TO 350°F. IN A
3 OR 4 QUART CASSEROLE ARRANGE THE
INGREDIENTS IN LAYERS; FIRST RICE, THEN
VEGETABLES, THEN RICE AGAIN, THEN ALL THE
MEAT (WHATEVER YOU USE), RICE AGAIN, VEGETABLES,
THEN THE REST OF THE RICE. POUR THE RESERVED
COOKING LIQUID OVER ALL AND DOT WITH BUTTER.
BAKE FOR AN HOUR OR SO, UNTIL RICE IS COMPLETELY
COOKED.

CONTINUED

GARNISH WITH ANY OR ALL OF THE FOLLOWING AND SERVE IN THE CASSEROLE.   THIS IS AN ENTIRE MEAL IN ONE DISH.

- SLIVERED ALMONDS (TOASTED)
- CUCUMBER SLICES
- CHOPPED DATES
- FRUIT OR BERRIES
- RAISINS
- AUTHENTIC EDIBLE GOLD OR SILVER FOIL OBTAINABLE IN EAST ASIAN GROCERY STORES, CALLED "VARK".

MADRAS EGG CURRY

HARD COOKED EGGS

PRESUMING THAT MANY PEOPLE HAVE A FEAR OF GRAY-GREEN TINGED EGG YOLKS I INCLUDE MY FOOLPROOF METHOD OF AVOIDING DISASTER.   IF YOU ARE ATTENTIVE AND DON'T PERMIT THE EGGS TO BOIL THEY WILL BE PERFECT.

8   NOT-TOO-FRESH EGGS *
1 1/2 QUARTS COLD WATER

COVER THE EGGS WITH COLD WATER IN A GOOD SIZED PAN.   BRING THE WATER TO A BOIL.   REMOVE FROM THE HEAT COVER THE PAN AND ALLOW THE EGGS TO SIT IN THE WATER FOR AT LEAST 12 MINUTES.   REFRIGERATE THE EGGS, IF YOU ARE NOT USING THEM IMMEDIATELY ~ AND BE SURE TO MARK THEM SO YOU CAN TELL WHICH ARE THE COOKED ONES.

BRASS FIGURE, VIZAGAPATAM

* FRESH EGGS ARE ALMOST IMPOSSIBLE TO PEEL.

CURRY

2	TBSP. OIL	1	TEASPOON SALT, OR TO TASTE
1	MEDIUM ONION, CHOPPED	1/4	CUP TOMATO PUREE
1	CLOVE GARLIC, CHOPPED FINE	1 1/2	CUPS WHEY OR WATER (PAGE 48)
1	3/4" CUBE FRESH GINGER, CHOPPED VERY FINE	1	LARGE FRESH TOMATO, CHOPPED
		1	TEASPOON GARAM MASALA (OPTIONAL)
1	TBSP. CURRY POWDER (SEE PAGE 16-17)	1	TBSP. FRESH PARSLEY, CHOPPED

HEAT THE OIL IN A WOK. SAUTÉ THE CHOPPED ONIONS, GARLIC, AND GINGER UNTIL SOFT AND SLIGHTLY BROWN.

ADD THE CURRY POWDER AND STIR AND FRY FOR ANOTHER MINUTE OR TWO. ADD SALT, TOMATO PUREE, WHEY, AND CHOPPED TOMATO AND BRING TO A SIMMER. COOK UNTIL FRESH TOMATO IS HOT. SPRINKLE WITH GARAM MASALA, IF YOU ARE USING IT, REMOVE FROM HEAT.

PEEL AND QUARTER THE EGGS, LENGTHWISE. ARRANGE IN A CASSEROLE OR SERVING DISH. POUR THE SAUCE OVER THE EGGS. GARNISH WITH CHOPPED PARSLEY AND SERVE IMMEDIATELY.

PEAS with PANEER

PANEER   MAKES 1/2 LB.

MAKING FRESH CHEESE IS AN EXCELLENT WAY TO USE "OLD" MILK THAT IS ABOUT TO TURN. YOU CAN ADD LEFT OVER WHIPPING CREAM, YOGURT, COFFEE CREAM, OR ANY AGING DAIRY LIQUID.

2	QUARTS WHOLE MILK (NON-HOMOGENIZED IF POSSIBLE)	1/2	CUP UNFLAVORED YOGURT
1/2	TEASPOON SALT, (OPTIONAL)	2	TEASPOONS LEMON JUICE

CONTINUED

BRING THE MILK AND SALT TO A BOIL IN A HEAVY-BOTTOMED SAUCEPAN, BEING CAREFUL NOT TO BURN IT OR ALLOW IT TO STICK TO THE PAN. REDUCE THE HEAT AND ADD THE YOGURT AND LEMON JUICE, COOKING AND STIRRING UNTIL THE CURDS SEPARATE FROM THE CLEAR, YELLOWISH WHEY.

MOISTEN A CLEAN DISH TOWEL OR OTHER POROUS CLOTH (IF YOU USE CHEESE CLOTH YOU WILL HAVE TO USE 4 LAYERS) AND PLACE IT IN A STRAINER OR COLANDER OVER A POT OR BOWL TO CATCH THE WHEY.

POUR THE CURDS AND WHEY INTO THE CLOTH AND ALLOW IT TO DRAIN AND COOL. WHEN COOL ENOUGH TO HANDLE, WRING AND PRESS THE CLOTH TO REMOVE AS MUCH WHEY AS YOU CAN. SCRAPE THE CHEESE FROM THE CLOTH WITH A RUBBER SPATULA AND PLACE IN A COVERED CONTAINER.

THESE SOFT CURDS ARE CALLED "CHENNA" AND CAN BE USED IN ANY RECIPE CALLING FOR COTTAGE CHEESE, RICOTTA, OR CREAM CHEESE.

TO MAKE PANEER THE CHENNA MUST BE PRESSED FURTHER TO REMOVE MORE MOISTURE. WRAP THE CHENNA IN A CLEAN, DRY CLOTH, FORMING IT INTO A LOAF OR PATTY OR WHAT YOU WISH. PLACE IT ON A THICK PAD OF NEWSPAPER OR ON AN INCLINED BOARD SO THAT THE MOISTURE WILL EITHER BE ABSORBED OR IT WILL RUN OFF. WEIGHT IT WITH A HEAVY OBJECT AND ALLOW IT TO STAND AT ROOM TEMPERATURE UNTIL IT FORMS A VERY FIRM CAKE. WRAP AND REFRIGERATE FOR FUTURE USE.

SAVE THE WHEY TO USE IN MAKING SOUPS, BREADS, HOT CEREALS, OR INSTEAD OF WATER IN SAUCES. IT HAS A DELIGHTFUL SOUR TASTE AND MAKES AN EXCELLENT BEVERAGE WHEN CHILLED.

PREPARING CHEESE

1	RECIPE PANEER
1/2	CUP (OR SO) OIL OR **USLI GHEE** FOR FRYING

CUT THE PANEER INTO 3/4" CUBES OR BITE-
SIZED PIECES AND COAT VERY LIGHTLY WITH FLOUR.
HEAT THE OIL OR GHEE IN A WOK OR SMALL DEEP-
FRYER AND FRY THE CUBES UNTIL NICELY BROWNED.
DRAIN ON PAPER TOWELS AND HIDE THEM, BECAUSE
ANYONE PASSING THROUGH THE KITCHEN WILL EAT
'EM ALL UP.

CURRY

2	TBSP. **GHEE** OR OIL	1	CUP CHOPPED FRESH TOMATOES <u>OR</u> 1/2 CUP TOMATO PUREE
1	CUP ONIONS, FINELY CHOPPED		
2	GARLIC CLOVES, MINCED VERY FINE	1/4-1/3	CUP WHEY OR WATER
1/4"	SLICE OF FRESH GINGER, MINCED VERY FINE	1	10 OZ. PACKAGE OF FROZEN PEAS, <u>OR</u> 1 1/2 CUPS FRESH PEAS
2	TEASPOONS GROUND CORIANDER	1	TEASPOON SALT (OR TO TASTE)
1	TEASPOON PAPRIKA	1	TEASPOON **GARAM MASALA**
1/2	TEASPOON TURMERIC	1	TBSP. CHOPPED PARSLEY (FRESH)
1/4	TEASPOON CAYENNE (OR TO TASTE)		

HEAT THE GHEE IN A WOK OR HEAVY FRY-PAN.
COMBINE THE ONIONS, GARLIC, AND FRESH GINGER
AND STIR AND FRY UNTIL THE ONIONS ARE SOFT AND
BEGIN TO BROWN. ADD THE CORIANDER, PAPRIKA,
TURMERIC, AND CAYENNE AND COOK, STIRRING, FOR
ANOTHER TWO MINUTES. ADD THE TOMATOES AND
COOK UNTIL THICKENED AND SOMEWHAT DRY.

ADD THE WHEY AND BRING TO A BOIL. THEN
ADD THE PEAS AND SALT TO TASTE. COOK UNTIL THE
PEAS ARE DONE. THIS DISH CAN BE MADE HOURS
BEFORE SERVING OR EVEN ON THE PREVIOUS DAY. IT
AGES WELL.

BEFORE SERVING, HEAT CURRY TO A SIMMER,
CAREFULLY FOLD IN THE CHEESE CHUNKS AND HEAT
THEM. SPRINKLE ON THE GARAM MASALA AND TURN
INTO A SERVING DISH. GARNISH WITH THE PARSLEY.

MIXED VEGETABLE RAITA

THIS IS AN EXCELLENT WAY TO USE LEFT OVER VEGETABLES.

2   CUPS COOKED MIXED VEGETABEES, CUT IN PIECES (BITE-SIZE)
2   TEASPOONS LEMON OR LIME JUICE
1   TEASPOON CELERY SEED
1/2 TEASPOON GARAM MASALA
SALT TO TASTE
1/2 CUP UNFLAVORED YOGURT

PLACE THE VEGETABLES IN A BOWL. MARINATE IN THE LEMON JUICE, CELERY SEED, GARAM MASALA, AND SALT FOR ABOUT 15 MINUTES. MIX LIGHTLY WITH YOGURT. REFRIGERATE UNTIL READY TO SERVE.

CARROT HALWA

SERVES 4-6

4   CUPS GRATED CARROTS
1   1" CINNAMON STICK
2   CUPS WATER
1/3 CUP HONEY, DATE SUGAR, BROWN SUGAR, OR JAGGERY

2   CUPS MILK
1/2 CUP GROUND ALMONDS
5 OR 6 CRUSHED CARDAMOM SEEDS
2   TBSP. USLI GHEE
1/4 CUP RAISINS

COOK THE GRATED CARROTS AND CINNAMON STICK IN THE WATER UNTIL THEY ARE SOFT AND ALMOST ALL OF THE WATER HAS EVAPORATED.

ADD THE SWEETENER AND MILK AND BRING TO A SIMMER. COOK UNTIL THICK AND FAIRLY DRY. ADD THE ALMONDS, CARDAMOM, GHEE, AND RAISINS AND COOK FOR ANOTHER MINUTE, STIRRING CONSTANTLY. REMOVE AND DISCARD THE CINNAMON STICK.

POUR INTO A GLASS BOWL AND GARNISH WITH SLIVERED ALMONDS AND A DASH OF NUTMEG. SERVE HOT, WARM, COOL, OR CHILLED, AS YOU LIKE.

Recipes For

MENU 5

KORMA CURRY

KITCHEREE

GREEN BEANS with COCONUT

CHAPATTIS

EGGPLANT RAITA

MADRAS HALWA

GLOSSARY

CHAPATTI — UNLEAVENED WHOLE WHEAT BREAD
SIMILAR TO MEXICAN TORTILLAS.

KITCHEREE — A COMBINATION OF RICE AND LEGUME,
COOKED TOGETHER WITH OR WITHOUT
SPICING. THE USUAL PROPORTION IS
FOUR PARTS RICE TO ONE PART LEGUME.

KORMA — A RICH SAUCED MEAT OR POULTRY STEW
ORIGINATING IN KASHMIR. RECIPES
OFTEN CALL FOR NUTS, COCONUT MILK,
AND YOGURT, AS WELL AS A VARIETY
OF SPICES, SEEDS, AND AROMATIC
VEGETABLES. THIS KIND OF CURRY
IS SUPERB WHEN TEMPEH OR FIRM
TOFU IS USED INSTEAD OF MEAT.

RAITA — VEGETABLE SALAD WITH YOGURT.

MADRAS — A PUDDING LIKE CONFECTION MADE WITH
HALWA FINELY MILLED CREAM OF WHEAT OR
FARINA. WHEN GROUND SO FINE IT IS
CALLED SEMOLINA FLOUR. THIS
VERSION IS SOUTH INDIAN.

KORMA CURRY

1 1/2	LBS. CUBED LAMB	1/4	CUP UNROASTED
1	TBSP. GARAM		CASHEW NUTS
	MASALA	1	TEASPOON SALT,
2	TBSP. WHITE POPPY		OR TO TASTE
	SEEDS	1	CUP WHEY OR
18	WHOLE ALMONDS		WATER (PAGE 47)
2"	STICK CINNAMON	1	LARGE ONION,
1	TEASPOON		CHOPPED
	TURMERIC	2	TBSP. OIL
1	TEASPOON	1/2	CUP UNFLAVORED
	PAPRIKA		YOGURT
1	3/4" CUBE FRESH	1/4	TEASPOON CAYENNE,
	GINGER		OR TO TASTE
6	CLOVES OF GARLIC	2	TBSP. OIL TO
			BROWN LAMB

CUBE LAMB INTO BITE-SIZED PIECES. COMBINE GARAM MASALA, POPPY SEEDS, ALMONDS, CINNAMON, TURMERIC, AND PAPRIKA IN A SPICE MILL AND GRIND TOGETHER. SET ASIDE.

COMBINE THE GINGER, GARLIC, CASHEWS, SALT, AND WATER IN A BLENDER OR FOOD PROCESSOR AND BEAT UNTIL VERY SMOOTH.

HEAT THE OIL IN A WOK AND SAUTÉ THE ONION UNTIL IT BEGINS TO BROWN. ADD THE DRY NUT/ SPICE MIXTURE AND STIR AND FRY FOR ABOUT A MINUTE. ADD THE BLENDED MIX AND THE YOGURT AND STIR UNTIL IT BEGINS TO THICKEN. IF IT BECOMES TOO THICK, ADD MORE WATER OR WHEY. POUR THE SAUCE INTO A 2 QUART CASSEROLE.

CLEAN THE WOK AND HEAT THE OIL. STIR AND FRY THE LAMB UNTIL IT IS BROWNED. TRANSFER TO THE CASSEROLE AND STIR TO COAT WITH SAUCE. BAKE, COVERED, IN A 350°F. OVEN 45 MINUTES UNTIL THE LAMB IS VERY TENDER.

KITCHEREE

1/4	CUP LENTILS OR	2 1/2	CUPS WATER OR
	OTHER LEGUME		WHEY
1	CUP RICE, ANY	1	TBSP. USLI GHEE
	KIND		
1/2	TEASPOON SALT		

WASH THE LENTILS AND RICE.
COMBINE WITH SALT AND WATER IN
A HEAVY-BOTTOMED SAUCEPAN WITH
A 1½ QUART CAPACITY. COVER
PARTLY AND BRING TO A BOIL.
REDUCE HEAT TO LOW, COVER TIGHTLY AND SIMMER
UNTIL BOTH GRAINS ARE SOFT TO YOUR TASTE.

IF YOU ARE USING A QUICK COOKING RICE,
BEGIN COOKING THE LEGUMES BEFORE ADDING THE
RICE. FOR EXAMPLE, IF THE RICE TAKES ONLY 10
MINUTES AND THE LEGUME TAKES 35 MINUTES,
COOK THE LEGUME FOR 25 MINUTES, THEN ADD THE
RICE.

CHECK FREQUENTLY AND ADD WATER OR WHEY
AS NEEDED. WHEN FULLY COOKED THERE SHOULD
BE NO WATER LEFT. ADD THE GHEE, FOLDING
LIGHTLY TO DISTRIBUTE EVENLY. SERVE VERY HOT.

SPICED KITCHEREE

1	CUP BROWN RICE	1	½" CUBE FRESH
¼	CUP LENTILS		GINGER
2½	CUP WATER OR	2	TBSP. **GHEE**
	WHEY	1-2	TEASPOONS **GARAM**
1	SMALL ONION		**MASALA**
1	CLOVE GARLIC		SALT TO TASTE

WASH THE RICE AND LENTILS WELL AND SOAK IN
COLD WATER WHILE YOU PREPARE THE OTHER
INGREDIENTS. BRING THE WATER TO A BOIL.

CHOP THE ONION, GARLIC, AND GINGER VERY FINE.
HEAT THE GHEE IN A SKILLET THAT HAS A TIGHT LID.
SAUTÉ THE CHOPPED VEGETABLES UNTIL SOFTENED.
ADD THE **GARAM MASALA** AND FRY ANOTHER MINUTE.

DRAIN THE RICE AND LENTILS WELL AND ADD TO
THE PAN. STIR AND FRY FOR A FEW MINUTES, UNTIL

CONTINUED

RICE GRAINS BEGIN TO LOOK OPAQUE. ADD THE
BOILING WATER OR WHEY.
    COVER TIGHTLY AND COOK OVER LOW HEAT
UNTIL THE MOISTURE IS ABSORBED, ABOUT 30
MINUTES. CHECK OFTEN TO SEE THAT IT DOES
NOT COOK DRY, ADDING MORE WATER AS NECESSARY.
    REMOVE FROM HEAT AND KEEP TIGHTLY COVERED
UNTIL SERVING TIME.

GREEN BEANS with COCONUT

1	LB. FRESH GREEN BEANS	1	TEASPOON BLACK MUSTARD SEEDS
1/4	CUP UNSWEETENED GRATED COCONUT	1/2	TEASPOON SALT
1/4	CUP WARM WATER	1	SMALL SEEDED GREEN CHILI PEPPER, CHOPPED FINELY
2	TBSP. USLI GHEE		

    CLEAN AND CUT THE GREEN BEANS INTO 2"
PIECES. COOK IN A STEAMER OR WITH A SMALL
AMOUNT OF WATER UNTIL SOFTENED TO YOUR TASTE.
    MIX THE COCONUT WITH THE WATER AND SET
ASIDE. HEAT THE GHEE IN A FRYING PAN AND FRY
THE SEEDS UNTIL THEY POP. ADD THE COOKED
BEANS, SALT, AND CHILI PEPPER, IF YOU ARE USING
ONE. STIR AND COOK UNTIL BEANS
ARE WELL COATED WITH COCONUT
AND SEEDS.

CHAPATTIS

MAKES 20 6" ROUNDS

2	CUPS WHOLE WHEAT PASTRY FLOUR OR 1 CUP WHOLE WHEAT AND 1 CUP UNBLEACHED WHEAT FLOUR	1/2	TEASPOON SALT, OPTIONAL
		2/3-1	CUP WARM WATER OR WHEY

54

MEASURE THE FLOUR AND SALT INTO A BOWL OR
INTO A FOOD PROCESSOR CONTAINER. ADD 1/2 CUP
WATER AND STIR VIGOROUSLY. ADD MORE WATER
WHILE STIRRING AND THEN KNEADING TO MAKE A
FAIRLY SOFT DOUGH.

TOSS ON A FLOURED BOARD AND KNEAD, AND
KNEAD, AND KNEAD UNTIL THE DOUGH IS VERY
ELASTIC AND SHINY.

THIS CAN BE DONE VERY SIMPLY IN A
PROCESSOR. WHEN THE DOUGH COMES
TOGETHER AND FORMS A SOFT BALL, RUN
THE PROCESSOR FOR ABOUT A MINUTE TO
KNEAD THE DOUGH.

WRAP THE DOUGH IN WAXED PAPER
AND A MOIST TOWEL, OR IN PLASTIC
WRAP AND ALLOW TO STAND AT ROOM
TEMPERATURE FOR ABOUT 1/2 HOUR.
DO NOT REFRIGERATE, UNLESS YOU
PLAN TO KEEP IT A LONG TIME.

KNEAD THE DOUGH LIGHTLY FOR
A FEW SECONDS AND FORM IT INTO
A CYLINDER ABOUT 10 INCHES LONG.
CUT THIS INTO 20 EQUAL PIECES
AND ROLL EACH INTO A BALL. KEEP THE BALLS IN A
PLASTIC BAG OR A CLOSED CONTAINER SO THEY WILL
NOT DRY WHILE YOU WORK WITH ONE AT A TIME.

HEAT AN IRON SKILLET UNTIL A DROP OF WATER
ROLLS AROUND. YOU MAY WIPE IT WITH OIL, IF YOU
WISH, BUT IT IS NOT NECESSARY. WORKING QUICKLY,
WITH ALL THREE HANDS, ROLL OUT A "CHAPATTI" ON
A FLOURED BOARD UNTIL IT IS VERY THIN AND ABOUT
6" IN DIAMETER. PLACE IT IN THE SKILLET AND
IMMEDIATELY START ROLLING THE NEXT ONE.
COOK EACH CHAPATTI FOR ABOUT 10 TO 12 SECONDS
ON EACH SIDE, UNTIL IT PUFFS AND SPOTS BECOME
DARK BROWN. PLACE THE BAKED CHAPATTI
IN A BASKET THAT HAS BEEN LINED WITH A
DISH TOWEL, AND REPEAT THE PROCESS.

THE TOWEL CAN BE MOISTENED
SLIGHTLY AND WRAPPED IN FOIL TO BE
REHEATED LATER, IF YOU WISH.

IF YOU WOULD LIKE TO WORK AT A
LESS FRENETIC PACE, YOU CAN ROLL ALL
THE CHAPATTIS, DUST THEM WITH FLOUR,
AND STACK THEM TO BE BAKED LATER.

CONTINUED

⁓ VARIATIONS

FOLLOWING THE PROCEDURE GIVEN ABOVE YOU CAN VARY THE DOUGH AS FOLLOWS:

1. ADD 2 TBSP. USLI GHEE OR OTHER SHORTENING TO THE DOUGH; USE SLIGHTLY LESS WATER.
2. USE 1½ CUP WHEAT FLOUR AND VARY THE OTHER ½ CUP WITH AMOUNTS OF CHICK-PEA FLOUR, LENTIL FLOUR, OR SOY FLOUR. USE SLIGHTLY MORE WATER WITH THESE HEAVY FLOURS.

EGGPLANT RAITA

PREHEAT OVEN TO 350°F.

1	MEDIUM EGGPLANT
2	TBSP. OIL
1	SMALL ONION, CHOPPED FINE
2	TBSP. CHOPPED SWEET GREEN PEPPER
2	TBSP. CHOPPED SWEET RED PEPPER
1	TEASPOON CELERY SEED
½	TEASPOON SALT
½-1	TEASPOON GARAM MASALA, TO TASTE
¾	CUP UNFLAVORED YOGURT
	LEMON JUICE

CUT THE EGGPLANT IN HALF. OIL THE CUT SIDE LIGHTLY WITH THE FINGERS AND PLACE FACE DOWN ON A BAKING SHEET. BAKE AT 350°F. UNTIL FAIRLY SOFT WHEN PIERCED WITH A FORK. REMOVE FROM THE OVEN AND COOL.

HEAT THE OIL IN A FRYING PAN OR WOK. SAUTÉ THE ONIONS UNTIL SOFT, DO NOT BROWN. ADD THE PEPPERS AND CELERY SEED AND FRY FOR SEVERAL MINUTES, UNTIL PEPPERS ARE SOFTENED.

PEEL AND CUT THE EGGPLANT INTO 1/2" CUBES.
ADD TO THE WOK WITH THE ONION AND PEPPERS AND
STIR AND COOK FOR A MINUTE OR TWO UNTIL COATED
WITH OIL.   ADD THE SALT AND GARAM MASALA, STIR,
AND THEN TURN INTO A BOWL TO COOL. SQUEEZE A
LITTLE LEMON JUICE OVER THE MIXTURE.
     WHEN COOL, FOLD IN THE YOGURT. REFRIGERATE
AND SERVE COLD.

MADRAS HALWA

1/2   CUP HONEY, **JAGGERY,**
       OR BROWN SUGAR
2   CUPS WATER
1/4 CUP RAISINS
       (OPTIONAL)
2   TBSP. WHITE POPPY
       SEEDS
6   CARDAMOM SEEDS

2   TBSP. UNSWEETENED
       COCONUT
2/3 CUP SEMOLINA OR
       FARINA
4   TBSP. **USLI GHEE**
1/4 CUP CHOPPED
       ALMONDS
       (OPTIONAL)

COMBINE THE SWEETENER, WATER,
AND RAISINS AND BRING TO A BOIL.
COMBINE THE POPPY SEEDS, CARDAMOM
SEEDS, COCONUT, AND ABOUT 2 TBSP.
SEMOLINA IN BLENDER OR SPICE GRINDER
AND GRIND VERY FINE. (IF USING FARINA
GRIND ALL OF IT).
     MELT THE USLI GHEE IN A WOK.   ADD
THE DRY MIXTURE AND STIR AND MIX
UNTIL VERY LIGHTLY BROWNED.   ADD THIS
TO THE BOILING SWEETENED WATER AND
BEAT VIGOROUSLY OVER HIGH HEAT UNTIL
THE MIXTURE BECOMES VERY THICK,
LEAVES THE SIDES OF THE PAN AND
BECOMES SHINY.   MIX IN THE
ALMONDS, IF YOU ARE USING THEM.
     SPREAD THIS MIXTURE IN A SQUARE
BAKING PAN, ABOUT 3/4" THICK.   COOL
AND CUT INTO SQUARES.   SPRINKLE
WITH POWDERED SUGAR AND DECORATE
WITH BLANCHED ALMONDS.

A SHORT DICTIONARY
of Curry Spices, Flavorings, and Pertinent Miscellany

Amchoor	Mango Powder, used to give a sour flavor. Lemon juice can be substituted.
Asafetida	A gum-resin of a plant of the carrot family, used in very small amounts, but essentially unnecessary. One source describes it as having an ". . . absolutely nauseating taste." Another says "This drug of ill savour . . ."
Bay leaf	Leaves of a tree native to the Mediterranean called Laurel or Sweet Bay. The California Bay tree has delightfully scented leaves which can also be used.
Black Pepper	Not to be confused with Capsicum (chili) peppers. Black peppercorns are the fruits of a tree (*Piper Nigrum*) believed native to the Malabar Coast of India.
Cardamon	Seeds of varieties of ginger plant, from which turmeric is also derived. The best is native to Southeast Asia. It is probably the second most expensive spice there is, the first being saffron. It is sweetly aromatic. Its most common American use is in baked goods and sausage. In India it is used in sweets and desserts as well as meat and rice dishes. Available in ground form in most supermarkets. Commercially ground cardamon usually includes the pod as well as the seed. It is less flavorful and much less expensive. Try to find whole seeds and grind them yourself.
Cashew Nut	Much enjoyed in Asian foods, it is used raw rather than roasted. Available in natural food stores.
Cayenne pepper, Chilies, Red pepper 	Members of the Nightshade family (*Solanaceae*), peppers of the species Capsicum from which "hot" pepper is derived contain a flavorless, insoluble chemical which burns the mouth, and to some, is absolutely unbearable. To others it is Nirvana. Believed to be native to Central and South America, the capsicum peppers were introduced to India in the 17th Century by the Portuguese and became very popular, especially in South India. It is thought that hot foods are popular in hot climates because they induce perspiration and increase thirst, which is supposed to cool the body. At one time it was suggested that people with cold feet wear socks dusted with red pepper. Cooks working with Capsicum peppers are advised to wear rubber gloves and avoid contact with the eyes. The seeds are especially offensive. If you do not like hot foods, curry dishes will not suffer by reducing the amount used or leaving them out entirely.
Cilantro	A member of the parsley family (*Umbelliferae*), also called Chinese parsley and very often confused with fresh coriander. Cilantro is pungent and much stronger than coriander. The English call it "fitweed" and "stinkweed." If you dislike the flavor, use parsley instead.

Cinnamon	The bark of a large evergreen of the Laurel family which grows wild in India and Sri Lanka. Used in both stick and ground form in some meat and rice dishes.
Cloves	Dried flower buds of a Southeast Asia evergreen. Very aromatic; used both ground and whole.
Coconut	The fruit of the *Cocos Nucifera*. It is very oily, oil which is highly saturated and not recommended for food purposes, although it, along with its companion palm kernel oils, is used extensively in confections, especially carob and chocolate. It has a property of remaining solid at fairly warm temperatures.
Coconut milk	This is made from ground coconut. It is *not* the liquid in the center of a fresh coconut, but is made from grated fresh or dried coconut mixed with water and strained. It imparts a delightful, sweet, subtle taste to foods. It is much used in South India.
Coriander (fresh)	A member of the parsley family (*Umbelliferae*) which includes fennel, anise, caraway, dill, and celery seeds. Widely used in Southeast Asian food, ground or whole.
Cumin	The fruit of an herb grown throughout Asia and used extensively in Mexican chili powder and in Southeast Asian food either whole or ground.
Dyhe (Dahi)	Milk curds very similar, if not identical to, yogurt. Very popular in India.
Fennel seeds	Similar in flavor to cumin, but much stronger. Anise seeds can be used interchangeably with fennel in some Indian foods. (see Coriander)
Fenugreek	An intensely aromatic leguminous seed (*Trigonelle foenum-graecum*) is used in most commercial curry powders. The cloying scent predominates, overpowering all other spices. It is the characteristic scent identified with curry. Although it is much used in Western versions of curry, it is less used in India, and not used at all in North Indian cuisine. It is said that it was and is widely used to mask the taste of spoiled meat. A tiny amount on the hands will linger for hours and can hardly be washed off. It can be omitted.
Garam Masala	A mixture of several spices. Translates to "hot spices." There are many recipes for this.
Ghee	Drawn butter or cooking oil. Butter is called *usli ghee*, meaning it is genuine butter. Vegetable oils are more widely used and also called *ghee*.
Ginger	The rhizome, or root of a group of plants native to Southeast Asia. (*Zingiberaceae*). Usually used fresh, but can be used in powder form as well.
"Hot" peppers, (Jalapeno)	Of the *Solanaceae*, these hot peppers are generally used green, before they become ripe. Red when ripe—and hotter, they are very popular in Mexico and California. One of the milder of the Capsicums. Can be bought canned. (See Cayenne)
Jaggery	An unrefined dark brown sugar made from the sap of coconut and Palmyrah palms. Use dark brown cane or beet sugar, maple sugar, or honey as a substitute. Jaggery is available in Indian markets.

Kari (Curry)	An ornamental shrub or tree that grows wild in India and Sri Lanka. The leaves are used in Indian food, but it is not used as part of commercial curry powder.
Lemon Grass	Used to impart a lemon flavor to curries. The plant yields an oil, citronella, used widely as an insect repellant. Genuine lemons are quite superior in flavor when part of the rind is also used.
Mace	A fleshy network that surrounds the nutmeg shell. One pound of mace is obtained from 400 pounds of nutmegs. Mace is similar in flavor to nutmeg, but milder and more subtle.
Masala	Any mixture of spices and flavorings, as varied as there are cooks to mix them. Make your own personal masalas soon.
Mint	Often added to rice and vegetable dishes and to chutneys.
Muglai	Meaning Mogul or Moghul; a style of cooking found mostly in Kashmir.
Mustard Seeds	Obtained from several plants of the crucifer family. (*Cruciferae*). Black seeds are used most widely in India. Yellow seeds will do as well.
Nutmeg	The seed of an evergreen native to the Moluccas. Can be used ground, but loses its zest quickly. Grate small amounts with a lemon rind grater or a special nutmeg grater. (See Mace)
Paprika	Made from sweet red peppers which are members of the Capsicum famiy. Generally ground without the seeds which can be very hot.
Roti	Breads of India, including chapatti, paratha, poori, luchi, generally unleavened and cooked on a griddle or deep-fried.
Saffron	The stigmas of the saffron crocus, a member of the Iris family, are much prized for their orange-red color and aromatic pungency. Saffron is enormously expensive, but a tiny amount goes a long way. (See Turmeric.)
Tamarind	The fruit of a large tropical tree used for its sour taste. It can be replaced by lemon juice. It is available in prepared form in Indian and Mexican food stores.
Tandoori	A barbecue cooked in a clay bee-hive shaped oven called a *tandoor*.
Turmeric	Also called "Indian Saffron," it is the rhizome of a plant of the ginger family. (*Zingiberaceae*). Dried and powdered, it is used instead of expensive saffron as a coloring agent, imparting the bright yellow-orange hue which is intimately associated with curries. It stains everything it comes in contact with. Its slightly bitter flavor will not be missed if it is not used.

Crocus. The stigmas of the *Crocus Sativus*, a plant of the natural order *Iridaceæ*, possess antispasmodic, stimulant, and emmenagogue properties; but they alone are not much to be depended upon. See *Saffron*.

CROCUS (SAFFRON)

botanical name, *Fœniculum Vulgaris*; it is valued chiefly for the aromatic and stimulant quality of its leaves and seeds, which are

also diuretic, and are useful in flatulency; the latter, and the oil extracted from them, are chiefly used; the dose of the Bruised Seeds is from 1 scruple to 3; of the Oil 2 or 3 drops; but it is generally taken in combination with other aromatics.

FENNEL

BIBLIOGRAPHY

1. Anwar, Zarinah. *With an Eastern Flavor*. New York: Barron's, 1979.
2. Chablani, Mohan and Brahm N. Dixit. *The Bengal Lancers Indian Cookbook*. Chicago: Henry Regnery Company, 1976.
3. Farb, Peter & George Armelagos. *Consuming Passions The Anthropology of Eating*. New York: Washington Square Press, 1980.
4. Hale, William Harlan and The Editors of Horizon Magazine. *The Horizon Cookbook*. American Heritage Publishing Co., 1968.
5. Harris, Diane. *The Cuisine of Northern India*. Bon Appetit, May 1980.
6. Jaffrey, Madhur. *An Invitation to Indian Cooking*. New York: Alfred A. Knopf, 1973.
7. Lie, Sek-Hiang. *Indonesian Cookery*. New York: Crown Publishing, 1963.
8. Lust, John. *The Herb Book*. New York: Bantam Books, 1974.
9. Morton, Julia F. *Herbs and Spices*. New York: Golden Press, 1976.
10. Rau, Santha Rama. *The Cooking of India*. New York: Time-Life Books, 1969.
11. Sahni, Julie. *Classic Indian Cooking*. New York: William Morrow and Company, Inc. 1980.
12. Stewart, John. *Kashmir*. Cuisine Magazine, February 1982.
13. Tannahill, Reay. *Food in History*. New York: Stein and Day, 1973.
14. *The Curry Mystery*, Sunset Magazine, February 1977.
15. *The Family Doctor: A Dictionary of Domestic Medicine and Surgery*. London: George Routledge and Sons, 1886.
16. Trager, James. *The Enriched, Fortified, Concentrated, Country-Fresh, Lip-Smacking, International, Unexpurgated Foodbook*. New York: Grossman Publishers, 1970.
17. Veerasawmy, E.P. *Indian Cookery*. Bombay: Jaico Publishing House, 1956.
18. Waldo, Myra. *The Complete Book of Oriental Cooking*. New York: Bantam Books, 1960.
19. Williams, Sue. *Nutrition and Diet Therapy*. Saint Louis: The C.V. Mosby Company, 1977.

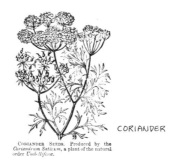

CORIANDER

CORIANDER SEEDS. Produced by the *Coriandrum Sativum*, a plant of the natural order *Umbellifera*.

INDEX

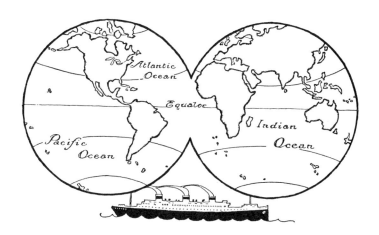

Juel Andersen's PRIMERS

THE TOFU PRIMER
A Beginner's Book of Bean Cake Cookery
Juel Andersen with Sigrid Andersen
Widely available now in supermarkets and natural food stores, tofu can also be made at home as illustrated in *The Tofu Primer*. An invaluable investment for everyone!
Illustrated   3.95

TOFU FANTASIES
A Collection of Incomparable Dessert Recipes
Juel Andersen
A gemlike collection of imaginative dessert recipes using tofu in ways wok chefs have never explored.
Illustrated   4.95

Juel Andersen's CAROB PRIMER
Robin Clute with Sigrid Andersen
The ABCs of using carob in delicious and healthful breads, muffins, and desserts. Carob is naturally sweet and highly nutritious, with *three times* as much calcium as milk, and a full complement of other minerals and B-vitamins.
Illustrated   3.95

Juel Andersen's TEMPEH PRIMER
Robin Clute with Sigrid Andersen
Tempeh: pronounce it "tempay," and use it as you would meat—in stews, sautées, loaves, and burgers. *Food Processing* magazine rated tempeh highest in taste, nutritional benefits and simple, low-cost processing techniques.
Illustrated   3.95

SEA GREEN PRIMER
Richard Ford
The *Sea Green Primer* tells how to prepare delicious meals from the more common sea weeds such as dulse and agar, and also introduces you to arame, hijiki, kombu, and wakame, all common in the Orient and now available in many supermarkets.
Illustrated   3.95

SESAME PRIMER
Juel Andersen
A delectable collection of recipes, a compilation of marvelous and mysterious uses, and a treasury of captivating illustrations.
Illustrated   3.95

CURRY PRIMER
A Grammar of Spice Cookery
Juel Andersen
An adventure into the mysteries of spice combining to delight the cook and charm the guest.
Illustrated   4.50

SEAFOOD PRIMER
A Practical Book of Fish Cookery
Shirley LaMere
Make high-nutrition, low-fat, delicious meals from ordinary, inexpensive fish.
Illustrated   4.50

Copies can be ordered from:
CREATIVE ARTS BOOK CO. 833 Bancroft Way, Berkeley, CA 94710
Please add $1.00 postage and handling, each additional book .50.